FROM PUMPKIN HOOK
TO DUMPLING HILL

FROM
PUMPKIN HOOK
TO
DUMPLING HILL

By ARCH MERRILL

Manufactured in 1969 by American Book–Stratford Press, Inc.,
75 Varick St., New York, N.Y. 10013
Address all orders and inquiries to
Creek Books, P.O. Box 9633,
Rochester, New York 14604

Contents

List of Illustrations

FROM PUMPKIN HOOK
TO DUMPLING HILL

Chapter 1

A Many-Sided Land

Not the least of Western-Central New York's charms is the diversity of its pattern.

Its scenery ranges from the spectacular to the pastoral. It houses Upstate New York's three largest cities. Its country-side is dotted with drowsy New Englandish hamlets, with here and there a "ghost town."

The region has produced statesmen, landed gentry, re-formers, promoters, eccentrics, daredevils and master criminals.

It also is a land abounding in picturesque place names. Hence the title of this opus: *From Pumpkin Hook to Dumpling Hill.* These and many more strange place names will be the subject of the next chapter. They point up the distinctive quality of this many-sided land.

As they thumb through these pages, some folks will say: "Why, I read this story in another Merrill book." Those people are so right. Most of the stories did appear in these earlier titles, now long out of print:

Tomahawks and Old Lace (1948); *Upstate Echoes* (1950) and *Shadows on the Wall* (1952).

1

The stories selected from the earlier regional books chronicle unusual and sometimes mysterious happenings and portray extraordinary people, such as the wealthy Yale graduate who patched his own clothes and lived a hermit's life.

There also are several chapters which were not included in earlier books. One bears the self-explanatory heading: "Cobblestone Country."

Many persons assisted in gathering material for this book. I note with sadness that several who gave generous help are no longer in the land of the living.

And so many readers showered me with queer place names that it is impossible to list them all. I must credit J. Sheldon Fisher of Fishers with first suggesting the collection of the unusual names and with contributing many of them.

My thanks also go to the Rochester Public Library, the Grosvenor Library in Buffalo and the Cornell University Library, as well as the DeWitt Historical Society in Ithaca and public libraries in Syracuse, Auburn, Palmyra, Marion and other communities.

This by no means complete list of acknowledgements must also include the names of Orleans County Historian Cary H. Lattin, York Town Historian Arthur B. Donnan, Cliff Spieler of the *Niagara Falls Gazette,* Raymond Yates of Lockport, Mrs. Marie Preston, Livingston County Historian, and her assistant, Miss Ann Patchett; Mrs. Eleanor C. Kalsbeck, Henrietta Town Historian, the Rev. Robert F. McNamara.

Chapter 2

Picturesque Place Names

You won't find Pumpkin Hook or Dumpling Hill on any official map. Like scores of other odd names in this region, they live only in the folklore of the land.

Pumpkin Hook is a nickname for the old Quaker settlement of Farmington in Ontario County. It is in the township still named Farmington but there's no longer a postoffice of that name. So the pleasant little community is generally called Pumpkin Hook or simply "The Hook."

Years ago, so the story goes, pumpkins were literally taken by hook out of fields there. Certainly they were "hooked" in the sense of being stolen.

It happens that the Finger Lakes race track is in the Town of Farmington but the sedate "Hook" is far enough away so that it never hears the roar of the grandstands.

Dumpling Hill is an eminence on the Scottsville Road along the Genesee River south of Rochester. It got its name because, 'tis said, a woman who lived there in a bygone day made the most succulent apple dumplings ever tasted.

3

Today it is the site of the large estate of the Wehle family, established by the late Louis A. Wehle, brewery magnate and prominent Democrat.

Tourists who never heard of Pumpkin Hook or Dumpling Hill are intrigued by such official community names as Horseheads, Painted Post, Penn Yan and Onoville. Back of each strange name is a story.

On a boulder in the Chemung County village of Horseheads is this inscription:

"In 1779 near this spot Gen. John Sullivan mercifully disposed of his pack horses worn out in the campaign against the Iroquois. The first white settlers entering this village in 1789 found the bleached skulls and named the place Horseheads."

In a distant day the Indians erected a massive painted oaken post where the Tioga and Conhocton Rivers unite to form the Chemung and where the trails forked. It was a landmark and a rendezvous in the forest empire of the Senecas. When the white men built a town there, they named it Painted Post. A monument in the public square of the Steuben County industrial village preserves the tradition.

The shire town of Yates County was settled by a mixture of Pennsylvanians and New Englanders. Each group wanted its home region recognized in the name of the village. A Solomon-like settler ended the dispute with a compromise name. He proposed: "Penn for the Pennsylvanians among us and Yan for the Yankees."

Onoville is a tiny place bordering the Cattaraugus In-

4

dian Reservation and just north of the Pennsylvania line. It was first dubbed Jugtown and residents considered that undignified. They called a meeting to pick a suitable name. Name after name was proposed. To each one some one would say: "Oh no, That won't do." Finally a wag spoke up: "Why not call it Onoville?" and Onoville it remains to this day.

Through the years peculiar names have clung to settlements, roads, hills, hollows and streams. Usually the names go back to early times. They were inspired by some trait of the inhabitants, some incident or natural formation. Often the names were bestowed in a spirit of derision.

The reason for the unusual place name or nickname in some cases has been lost in the mists of time. For years my native village of Sandusky, Cattaraugus County, bore the nickname of Henpeck. The same sobriquet was given Elmgrove or South Greece in Monroe County. Why nobody seems to know.

Besides Dumpling Hill, places with gastronomical connotations include Hungry Hollow, west of Hammondsport; Round Pie Station (Conesus) where the station agent's wife made little round pies which were sold to passengers at five cents each; Sweetcake Hollow, near Nunda; Johnny Cake Lane in Orleans County and Johnny Cake Lane, now Mile Square Road, in eastern Monroe County.

There are two Molasses Hills, one near Alexander and another near Nunda, as well as a Molasses Corners on the

5

outskirts of Canandaigua. All figured in spilled barrels of molasses.

On Nutty Hill, in the Victor area, chestnut and hickory groves once flourished. The several Pumpkin Hills were so named because of their shape. The most famous one is on the Wells College campus at Aurora. There's Goose Corners in the Nunda vicinity.

After the War of 1812 a settlement sprang up at a crossroads south of Le Roy. An early industry was a distillery and its proprietor set up a liberty pole with a little brown jug at its top to advertise his wares. Now only a cemetery is left at Jug City.

All trace of the Kingdom, a flourishing community in the early 19th Century just west of Seneca Falls, is vanished. The name possibly was a corruption of King's Dam.

In the Town of Mendon was a Black and White Corners, so called because the Whites lived on one corner and a Negro family on the other.

One version of the origin of the name of Belcoda in the Town of Wheatland is that when a church was being built a confused settler called its belfry a "belcody." The other is that was named for a Miss Belle Cody.

The only place on the frontier for miles around where there was plenty of corn was the settlement which the pioneers, remembering the Biblical story, named Egypt.

The name of Golah, a onetime railroad station in Rush, was formed from the first initials of the names of five families in the neighborhood.

A place on the Erie Canal near Lyons was known as

Pilgrimport after a fanatical religious group pitched its tents there.

There are several Podunks and Podonques, the best known of which is Podonque near Ithaca. And in the vicinity of Arcade you will find a Punkshire.

It is questionable whether some communities would wish to have their original names or nicknames restored, although Hemlock has perpetuated its old name, Slab City, in promoting its "World's Fair."

Perry began life as Slabtown, then became Shacksburg. North Bloomfield was Puppytown. Orleans was Hardscrabble. Phelps was Woodpecker City. Manchester was Coonsville. Because its ladies were given to the use of snuff, East Victor was Snufftown. Peg Town, where shoe pegs were made, now is a part of Hammondsport.

The west side of Cohocton was called Tripp's Corners, because in a brawl in a bar there, three Tripp brothers took on all comers and knocked them all out. South Bradford was known as Cat's Head because three roads converged there in the shape of a cat's head.

Houghton, the seat of a Wesleyan college of that name, is one of the few college towns where neither alcoholic drinks nor tobacco are sold. But years ago, when it was a tough port on the Genesee Valley Canal, it was called Jockey Street because of the Sunday horse racing and betting there.

The "feuding and fighting" of bygone years are reflected in some place names, along with other rather sinister connotations.

On the Middlesex Valley side of Canandaigua Lake is Rumpus Hill, the scene of incessant feuding which resulted in barn burnings and other unneighborly acts.

Dansville has a Battle Street. In Genesee Valley Canal days it was the scene of a struggle between villagers, who dug a slip from the canal to the center of the town, and the forces of the state who tried to stop them from letting the water into it. The townspeople won the battle. The old name, Battle Street, abandoned for a time, has been restored.

There's a Bloody Hollow near the Wyoming-Livingston county line because in Civil War times an inebriate smashed the windows of his brother-in-law's house with stones and was slain as a result.

The village with the appealing name of Friendship once was called Bloody Corners or Fighting Corners. And, believe it or not, Pleasant Valley years ago was known as Hell's Hollow.

North of Naples is a Feather Street. There two women tussled over the ownership of a feather bed. A strong wind blew feathers down the road for a considerable distance.

Men from the hills on either side of a valley used to stage rough games in a valley north of Hammondsport. The men of the northerly hill were usually victors and hence were called "bullies" by their rivals. That's how Bully Hill got its name.

Near Bath is a Gallows Hill, where a murderer was hanged in bizarre fashion. The masked executioner, all in black, galloped up to the gallows, pulled the rope and then dashed away. His identity was never revealed.

The Turk Hills are framed against the eastern sky in Monroe County. Years ago that range housed a band of squatters so lawless they were called "The Turks." They finally were ejected.

Between Conesus and Webster's Crossing lived the wild Caleboguers in a now extinct settlement. Some hold that the name is of Indian origin. Others assert that a saw mill operator named Caleb Bogue imported these lawless folk from the Hudson Valley.

Bogus Point on Lake Ontario and Bogus Corners near Hammondsport are legendary haunts of counterfeiters. Swindler's Gap is in the Bristol Hills. Rogues Harbor is on the eastern shore of Cayuga Lake near Ithaca. There are several Smugglers' Coves.

Poke o'Moonshine, meaning sack of liquor, is in the rough hills of the Wayland-Dansville area. Brandy Bay is an arm of Keuka Lake. Canandaigua Lake, not to be outdone, has a Whiskey Point. In the Town of Gainesville the memory of an old distillery is preserved in Whiskey Road. Inevitably cider and vinegar were made at Apple Jack, southeast of Victor.

Years ago there lived on the West Ridge near the Manitou Road an old woman who had an overweening curiosity about her neighbors' doings. Whenever she saw the doctor driving by, she would run to the door and call out: "Who's sick?" Whereupon the rise of ground on which her home stood became Hoosic Hill.

9

Before the Syracuse University campus was dubbed Piety Hill, an eminence on the Victor-Egypt Road bore that name because of the church that stood there.

In the Town of Victor are hills full of craters left by the retreating glaciers. They reminded the pioneers of food hoppers, hence the name, Hopper Hills.

Between Wyoming and Warsaw is a series of mounds, each divided by a ravine and known locally as the Giants' Graves.

In the Bliss-Gainesville area was Toddwaddle, a now extinct hamlet. It got its name in the 1840s because of a resident whose given name was Todd and whose gait was a waddle.

Tip Top near Alfred is the logical name for the highest point on the Erie Railroad. It has an altitude of 1,776 feet.

There is a Woodchuck Hill, a Bald Hill, a Potash Hill, a Wintergreen Hill in Palmyra, a Buttermilk Hill in the Town of Farmington, a Peacock Hill near Honeoye Falls, a Cobbler's Knob in the Bristols, a Pigeon Hill near Delevan and a Blue Hill in the same Town of Yorkshire, Cattaraugus County. In the upland lakes are the Marrowback and Whaleback ranges. Near my native village was a Dummy Hill where a family of deaf mutes lived.

In the Town of Sodus is a Christian Hollow, known locally as Christian Holler. It is said that in the 1840s when some Millerites gathered there to await the end of the world and when at the appointed hour the trump of doom failed to sound, a waggish fellow remarked: "You should have heard them Christians holler!"

The old Lower Fishers Road ran through a marsh where so many rigs became mired that women got out and tiptoed around it. The brambles ruined so many hoop skirts that the spot was called Hoop Skirt Hollow.

At Dark Hollow the ghost of a slain peddler is said to walk on moonlit nights. Also in the Bloomfields country are Spook Hollow, Frost Hollow, Skunk Hollow, Dutch Hollow and Factory Hollow, once an industrial center but now only part of the landscape.

Bootjack Hollow is near Hammondsport. Nearby is Birdseye Hollow at the head of Indian Run. Punky Hollow is near Naples. There are several Hog Hollows.

Shanty Plains is in the Guyanoga Valley near Branchport and Whetstone Creek is in the Bristols.

In the highway category are unusual names galore.

Dansville has a narrow block-long street officially marked Paradise Alley. It was named for a popular song of long ago.

Shirt Tail Bend was the name of an orphaned section of a street in Nunda which was separated from the main part of the artery by the Genesee Valley Canal. The "shirt" is on one side of the canal bed and the "tail" on the other.

Nunda also had a Tin Pot Alley, probably the present Center Street. Geneva has a street officially designated as Tin Can Alley. Tin Pot Corners is south of Albion.

There are two Stoney Lonesome Roads, one in the Bristol Hills and the other in the Mendon area. Hoe-handle Road is shaped like the farm tool, straight with a crook at one end. It's near Gainesville. On the Break of Day Road near Victor was a carriage shop whose operator always told customers he would be open for business at the break of day.

Other odd highway names: Zig Zag Road, east of Albion; Sawdust Road near Wayland and Pucker Street and Slickers Hill Road around Conesus; Pole Bridge Road near Avon; Bull Saw Mill Road in Mendon; Monkey Run, now the Valentown Road.

Nations Road in the fox-hunting country near Geneseo and the "Seven Nations," settled by people of many bloods; Basket Road in Webster, once known for its basket makers. Bear Swamp Road is near Pultneyville, Mudmills Road in the Newark area. And near Fillmore is a Goodenough Road.

Pre-emption Road in the Geneva region marks the boundary of the land to which Massachusetts was granted pre-emptive rights (the privilege of first purchase from the Indians.)

A road that leads to Rochester's Durand Eastman Park bears the regal name of King's Highway. Once it was the Hog's Back.

County House Road near the Wayne County Home at Lyons revives memories of a time when the almshouse was called "the County House" or worse still, the "Poor House." The several Plank Roads are also reminders of a day when highways were made of planks.

Strangest of highways is the Promised Land Road near

Olean. On a stretch of highway leading from Weston's Mills the traveler gets the impression he is going down hill when actually he is going up. It is an optical illusion caused by the contour of the land.

One of the most unusual place names around Rochester is Birds and Worms. It is said that a century ago young Rochester blades used to get up at dawn for a game of ball. When sides were chosen after a player remarked: "The early bird gets the worm," it was agreed that the winners would be called "early birds" and the losers "unfortunate worms." Out of that evolved a sportsmen's club and the bayside spot known as Birds and Worms.

Along Lake Ontario in the western corner of Monroe County is a wild, shaggy headland with treacherous shoals, for years the bane of mariners who warn: "Beware of the Devil's Nose."

Float Bridge once really floated. It was anchored to the shore by a chain. Methodist Hill was the scene of early meetings of the denomination before a house of worship was built. Rattlers once sunned themselves on Rattlesnake Point along the lower Genesee. Paddy Hill, on which stands Our Mother of Sorrows Church, got its name from its Irish settlers. Powder Mill Park was the site of a plant that made blasting powder.

Linked to the Indian lore of the countryside is tiny Squaw Island at the foot of Canandaigua Lake, the legendary hiding place for Seneca squaws and children during the Sullivan invasion, and the White Woman's Spring at Squawkie Hill, site of an old Indian village south of

Mount Morris. There Mary Jemison, the famed "White Woman of the Genesee," who lived with the Indians, came for water.

Bare Hill, which towers above the east side of Canandaigua Lake, is traditionally the birthplace of the Seneca Nation, although some authorities on Indian history insist that South Hill or Sunnyside should have that honor.

For years Lake Ontario has been carving out of the shore east of Sodus Point the tall, massive pillars, some of them fantastically shaped, which are known as Chimney Bluffs.

And there's the aptly named Jump-Off, the awesome chasm below Gannett Hill, the highest point in the Bristols.

Mystery surrounds the Lost Nation, a deserted tract in the northwestern corner of Allegany County. Romanticists like to believe it was the home of a lost tribe of Indians. There is more basis for the story it was a hideout for a gang of horse thieves. Now it is just so much abandoned farm land.

The Maygog is a curious name for a muckland and marsh in the Town of Macedon. Its suction has pulled several farm animals to their deaths, according to local tales. Maygog was the name of a mythical British ogre. Perhaps some scholar named the Wayne County Maygog.

In the name of all that's holy, why, because the first settler there was a Tory squatter named Poag, should a sylvan glen in the lordly hills above Dansville be encumbered with the horrid name of Poag's Hole?

14

Chapter 3

Cobblestone Country

Western-Central New York is America's "Cobblestone Country."

It is the cradle of a distinctive type of architecture. The cobblestones are relics of the glacial age but it was not until after 1825 that they were first used for the walls of the hundreds of houses, churches, schools, stores, sheds, barns and other structures that dot the countryside. Few were built after 1860.

Within a 100-mile radius of Rochester is by far the heaviest concentration of cobblestone buildings in the land. And there are more of the picturesque structures on the Ridge Road than on any other highway in America.

They are scattered over the Finger Lakes region and the Genesee Valley. They are fewer east of Syracuse. Outside of Upstate New York, there are some cobblestone houses in Canada's Ontario province, in Michigan and in Ohio. Some of these were built by former Western New Yorkers and probably all were inspired by the cobblestone masonry developed in this region.

We who grew up with these sturdy links with our past have, until recently, taken them too much for granted. We have allowed far too many fine specimens go the way of covered bridges.

In 1960 the Cobblestone Society was organized in Western New York with its paramount aim, "to preserve and protect our cobblestone heritage." It was an outgrowth of a movement by local residents to save a cobblestone church on the Ridge at Childs, near Albion. Now it has 350 members, including several from other states. The impressive accomplishments of the Society within a short time will be told later in this chapter.

In 1944 Carl F. Schmidt, Scottsville's architect-historian, wrote a book titled "Cobblestone Architecture." For the technical aspects of the subject, I have relied on that informative work and a brochure of more recent date by Miss Gerda Peterich, former associate researcher at Eastman House in Rochester, who recently retired from the art history and photography staff of Syracuse University. Schmidt illustrated his book with sketches, an art form that has won him wide recognition. Miss Peterich's six-page work contains several of her splendid photographs.

Schmidt's general description of cobblestone buildings follows:

"Cobblestone houses are sturdy, compact structures, built of small stones, laid up neatly, in horizontal rows between straight lines of exceedingly hard mortar, with square cut quoins of red and gray stones at the corners, giving an impression of dignity and solidity. Due to the materials, which are local, of warm and colorful tones, the structures appear to have grown from the soil on which they stand."

That tells the story succintly and vividly.

The earliest cobblestone houses were made of squarish "glaciated" fieldstones, irregular in shape, size and color, picked up from the fields. Schmidt wrote evidence points to the Henrietta-Mendon-Farmington area as the cradle of cobblestone masonry.

There is a local tradition that masons who worked on the locks of the Erie Canal stayed to build the cobblestone houses and settled in the fertile countryside. The buildings were the work of many hands, although in some areas many obviously were built by the same mason.

Other buildings were constructed of water-washed stones of greater uniformity of size and shape, found in gravel pits, fields and along Lake Ontario. Some of these structures are combinations of cobble and field stones. The smaller, rounder stones are plentiful around the Ridge Road, the wave-built natural highway which formed the shoreline of the great glacial Lake Iroquois.

Teams of oxen and horses hauled on wagons and stone boats many loads of lakeside stones into the interior, sometimes as far as 60 miles.

Some builders insisted on stones of uniform size, shape and color. These stones were graded for size by being passed through an iron ring or holes cut in a board. This uniformity made for a more monotonous, less colorful pattern than the other techniques.

A herringbone style was also produced, with longer stones laid at angles rather than in narrow rows.

Cobblestone buildings are of Post Colonial, Greek Revival and Victorian architecture with the Greek Revival predominating. Some have handsome doorways, a subject on which Schmidt is an authority. He divides the history of cobblestone building into three periods, merely as an aid in describing how they were built. He admits that the time periods are elastic and that a building of 1840 may look exactly like one fashioned a decade earlier.

Miss Peterich classifies the structures according to building techniques and geography. She wrote that strong regional variations may be found in patterns and color schemes because the materials came from the same neighborhood.

She reported that the prevailing color along Lake Ontario and East Ridge Road is brownish-red; that those west of Rochester are pinkish red, combined with gray, and in the region to the south the buildings are mostly yellow gray. Use of local limestone is general throughout the cobblestone country.

Names of some cobblestone masons have been preserved but little is known about where or how they were trained in their craft. Many of them guarded their formula jealously. Some of them even refused to let anyone watch them at work.

It took two to three years to build some cobblestone houses. Could one be reproduced today? Is cobblestone masonry a lost art, buried with the men who wielded the trowels? Schmidt wrote that he had reproduced several walls. A craftsman said only the length of time and expense involved could prevent a skilled mason from building one today.

Not only have too many cobblestone houses been removed from the scene but many have been marred by the addition of wooden lean-tos and incongruous frame porches.

In Rochester, center of "the Cobblestone Country," I could find but one of the distinctive buildings standing. It's referred to by Schmidt as the Lockwood House and is at Culver Road and Grand Avenue.

A fine specimen of cobblestone architecture was the house which stood for nearly a century at Main Street East and Culver Road and was for years the home of the late Detective Captain John P. McDonald, a rock-like character.

The oddest cobblestone structure I have ever seen is the former blacksmith shop at Alloway on the Lyons-Geneva Road. It has eight sides. Once years ago it was painted red, white and blue by the loser of an election bet, according to Wayne County's Historian, Mrs. Dorothy S. Facer of Lyons.

A cobblestone store in the heart of Victor has always intrigued me, as have the several large farm dwellings south of Phelps.

Still attractive is the house built in 1835 by P. P. Bonesteel on the Pittsford-Victor Road. Its owner described the building of the homestead for a farm magazine. He "used the common stone lime, one bushel of lime to seven of sand" and "furnished all materials on the ground."

He paid his masons $3.75 per 100 feet, boarded them, furnished his own tenders and made his own mortar. While he never kept an exact count on costs, he considered a cobblestone house, "the neatest and cheapest building that could be made." He pointed out it did not need painting.

At least nine cobblestone churches in the region were built and used for years. Now only the First Baptist Church in Webster and one in Alton remain as houses of worship. The others are vacant or diverted to other uses.

An eye-catching edifice is the Webster church, dedicated in 1857, with its shining dome supported by eight Corinthian pillars. It was built of small lake-washed sandstone cobbles. It houses a pipe organ which originally cost $100,000 and which graced the Chapin mansion in Rochester before it was razed for the Civic Center.

Once cobblestone district schools were as common as blacksmith shops in the area but so far as I can learn, not one of them is still "a temple of learning." One of the last to be abandoned was the one just north of Scottsville on the road to Rochester. It now is the Town of Chili Museum and houses a reproduction of an old time school. Except for special occasions, it is open only by appointment.

Many of the old schools have been converted into residences, some of them attractive, others spoiled by frame additions or other alterations. Some are vacant.

Opposite the old Bonesteel home near Victor is a handsome residence, once a schoolhouse. Another fine example of a remodeled school is the cobblestone house at Pultneyville across from the old Union Church.

And now to tiny Childs on the Ridge Road and its cluster of cobblestone buildings—a church, a schoolhouse, and three houses—all on the north side of the highway.

It was preservation of the distinctive Universalist Church, built in 1836, which spurred the organization of the Cobblestone Society, in October, 1960.

The general objectives of the society are not only "to preserve and protect our cobblestone heritage," but to operate as a non-profit educational and historical institution any buildings the society may acquire; to preserve and restore the cobblestone art in Childs, to establish a museum and library, to aid cobblestone structure owners in preserving and restoring their property, to increase public interest in cobblestone architecture and to unite all those interested in preserving them.

Robert Frasch, then a school teacher in the area, now on the staff of the Rochester Museum, conceived the idea of establishing Childs as "a cobblestone museum village reflecting life in the second quarter of the 19th Century."

Local residents concentrated first on the church and school. When it was found that the one-room school of District No. 5, built in 1849 and closed in 1952, was available, the society purchased it in 1961 for $129.

In 1963 the Cobblestone Society obtained title to the church and embarked on a repair and restoration program.

John D. Brush of Rochester, formerly of Albion, had the bell tower rebuilt and installed a 1,700-pound bronze bell in memory of his mother.

A growing museum collection is housed in the basement of the old church.

In the schoolhouse the past has come to life. The old slanting floor, wooden desks, blackboard, the teacher's desk and chair, even the maps and pictures on the wall are just as they were in bygone days.

Thanks to donors, many of them former pupils, the little room contains such remembered objects as a common waterpail and dipper, wash basin and towel, a globe let up and down from the ceiling by means of a rope, a collection of well worn text books, including McGuffey's Readers and old merit cards. In the "entry" are the hooks on which children hung their wraps.

And on many afternoons, young feet again cross the worn old threshhold and young voices echo in the yard at recess time.

For here a working museum-school is in session for third, fourth and fifth graders from schools in the area, some from Rochester suburbs.

J. Howard Pratt, the spry 78-year-old vice president of the Cobblestone Society and Gaines Town Historian, who once taught in district schools, calls the roll. He tells the children how the cobblestone school house was built and what school was like in bygone days. The school session is Pratt's idea and attracts more and more pupils each year.

The Society also has acquired the abandoned cobble-

2. Cary Lattin Residence near Albion, Built 1844

1. Eight-Sided Cobblestone Blacksmith Shop

stone schoolhouse at Gaines, just west of Childs on the Ridge Road. This building is used for storage and is the scene of a country auction each Autumn.

For the past eight years the organization has conducted tours of cobblestone buildings and other historic landmarks in various areas. Valuable publicity, as well as revenue, results from these annual pilgrimages.

In the Book of Proverbs, it is written: "Remove Not the Ancient Landmarks." That injunction includes cobblestone buildings, which represent a type of architecture cradled in and virtually peculiar to this many-sided Upstate land.

Chapter 4

Sails in the Sunset

*"Ships went to sea and ships came home from the sea,
And the slow years sailed by and ceased to be"*

———

Spring had come late to Pultneyville that year of 1825. But now the last ice had melted from Lake Ontario and the schooners seemed to strain at their moorings in the harbor, like race horses waiting the starter's bell.

In the ballroom of the tavern, many feet tripped to the brave music of the fiddles. It was the night of the Sailors' Farewell. In the Fall there would be the dance of the Sailors' Return.

For in 1825 Pultneyville was an important port and nearly all her men were sailing men. The sailors' eyes were bright as they danced. Their thoughts were of the morrow when they would hoist the white sails again and renew their age-old battle with wind and wave.

The eyes of the women who danced so lightly hid unshed tears. They were thinking of the long days ahead, the stormy days when they would go down to the water's

24

edge and peer out into the mists for the sight of sails long overdue. They were thinking of the sleepless nights to come when the gales would beat upon the snug white houses—and women could only worry and wait.

For there were so many sailing men who danced in the Spring and never came home to dance in the Fall.

The women recalled the fate of the schooner *Atlas* which had sailed out of Pultneyville the Autumn before with beef and pork for Kingston across the lake. The owners of the cargoes, some of the best men of the village, had gone along to sell their goods. A sudden storm and blinding snow swept down the St. Lawrence, the *Atlas* was driven on the rocks of Mexico Bay and never a man returned.

Doubtless young Horatio Nelson Throop, named after a great sea captain, was at the sailors' farewell ball. He was only 17 but his thoughts were all of ships and sailing men. His father, Samuel, a founder of the village, had been the first of a long line of Pultneyville sailing masters. He had launched the *Farmer,* a schooner of "30 tons burthen" in 1810. The next year it was driven aground and lost. Samuel Throop built another ship, the *Nancy.* In 1819 during a storm off Sodus Point, he was washed off its deck and drowned.

His son, Horatio, was then only 12. At 13 he was building his own boat, a small one, with the aid of a friendly ship's carpenter. Now in 1825 he was working on a larger one, one he was to command two years later, the youngest captain on the lake.

The ship sank on one of her first voyages. Her cargo of corn became damp and swelled, bursting a hole in her side. Three of the crew were lost and the young captain clung to a cabin door in a rough sea four hours before he was washed ashore.

Horatio Throop was to build and sail many another craft and eventually to become the leading skipper of Pultneyville. When the passenger steamboats came, he commanded the *Ontario,* pride of the lake, for years.

The name of Horatio Throop is on the stone memorial at the lakeside with the other 23 lake captains and the names of their ships. Now he sleeps with the other sailing men and boat builders, with his brother, Washington; the Ledyards, the Whipples, the Todds and the rest, in the old Lake View Cemetery overlooking the lake they knew so well.

Now only pleasure craft sail out of Pultneyville. The warehouses and mills that once lined Washington Street are gone; even the piers have rotted away.

Ghosts walk that old waterfront. Some of them walk with a rolling gait. There are frailer figures, the shawled women, their eyes swollen with weeping. They watch for ships that never will come home.

Chapter 5

From Genesee to Tennessee

This is a Genesee-Tennessee story. It revolves about one of the most remarkable personalities any region ever knew.

His name was Elisha Johnson. He was a pioneer, a rugged individualist, a daring promoter who built railroads and canals and had his finger in many pies.

He helped to mold Rochester from a frontier settlement into a boom town. He was the city's fifth mayor and he gave Rochester the public square which is an oasis in its heart.

Yet in Rochester he is a forgotten man. The mill race he dug in 1817 lasted 140 years before it went the way of the other raceways in this old flour milling town.

Johnson Street, a one-block artery he gave the city, has been swallowed up in the extension of Broad Street.

Washington Park, the shady square where the brooding figure of Lincoln crowns the Civil War monument, is a haven for hippies and pigeons. Only students of local history remember the name of its donor.

In the Valley of the Genesee amid the scenic glory of

Letchworth State Park there is a hole in the side of the rocky river gorge, now the home of thousands of bats, that is a reminder of this man's engineering failure of long ago. Nothing is left of the fantastic four-story log house he built beside the tossing Portage waters.

In the mountains of Eastern Tennessee there are the mansion he built and the ruins of his iron foundry which Sherman destroyed in 1865.

The story also involves a duel, a young man's flight from the law and an old man's new life in the Southland.

Elisha Johnson, a native of Vermont, educated at Williams College and the son of a Chautauqua County pioneer, came to the Genesee Country in 1812, at the age of 27 and settled at Canandaigua.

In 1817 he moved to the infant village Nathaniel Rochester had laid out beside the falls of the Genesee. He bought 80 acres from Enos Stone for $10,000, not on Rochester's 100-Acre Tract, but on the east side of the river. Johnson believed in the future of the East Side and was its first promoter. Like another Elisha, he was something of a prophet.

The year he came to Rochester he built a dam across the Genesee at the old fording place near the present Court Street bridge and dug a raceway from the dam to Main Street. Thereby he and his partner, Orson Seymour of Canandaigua, acquired valuable water rights in a potential flour-milling center. He envisioned mills along the Johnson-Seymour race, which was filled in only 10 years ago.

Johnson built his house on Clinton Avenue near the

street which bore his name. In 1821 he donated the land for the eastern half of the Aqueduct which carried the Erie Canal across the Genesee. In 1824 he had the contract to build a new Main Street bridge, replacing the primitive span over which troops had marched in the War of 1812. He built the Globe Building on the east side of the bridge and led the movement for a public market there.

The versatile and restless promoter plunged into many enterprises in the wake of the boom that followed the completion of the Erie Canal. He made maps of the young city and one of them was used in the first Rochester directory. He surveyed the site of Carthage, the settlement that sprang up on the east side of the Genesee south of the Ridge Road and was briefly a rival of Rochester.

He was a promoter and builder of the curious horse-drawn railroad which was completed in 1833 and for a decade linked Rochester and Carthage.

When the Iron Horse arrived on the scene, Johnson linked his fortunes to the newcomer. He was the contractor and chief engineer for Western New York's first railroad, the Tonawanda, which began operations on a single track of wooden rails between Batavia and Rochester in 1837. He was in charge of constructing a railroad from Toronto to Detroit.

He also was an inventor and in 1835 patented a new method of laying railroad tracks.

He found time for community endeavors. He was one of the organizers and the first vestryman of St. Paul's Episcopal Church. He gave the land for the First Methodist

Church on what is now South Avenue. He was a trustee of the Franklin Institute, an early literary and scientific society.

He served three terms as president of the village in late 1820s. In 1838 a Democratic Common Council chose Johnson as Rochester's fifth mayor. He served only one year, for the Whigs came into power in 1839. During his brief tenure, Mount Hope Cemetery was developed. Mayor Johnson advocated building of a city hall and submitted a comprehensive waterworks plan to replace private wells. Neither proposal was adopted. Johnson was generally ahead of his times.

His most enduring contribution to Rochester was his gift of the site of Washington Square. Its original trees were part of the primeval forest.

After 1838, when he took the contract to build the Portage section of the Genesee Valley Canal, Rochester knew colorful Elisha Johnson no more.

The canal project was a challenge to his engineering skill. It involved circumventing the falls of Portage by digging a tunnel through the massive rock barrier on the east side of the Genesee gorge. The state plans called for a tunnel 1,100 feet long, 27 feet wide and 20 feet high.

Tunnel builder Johnson ran into snags right away. Rock slides and quicksand hampered his diggers. After a dozen workmen had been killed by falling rock, the project was abandoned. It had cost the state $250,000.

Then the resourceful Johnson conceived the idea of swinging the canal around the mountain and pinning the waterway to the side of the cliff, no small feat in those days of hand labor. The rock was blasted away by black powder. It took 20 years to complete the canal from the Genesee in Rochester to the Allegany at Olean.

A hole in the rocky wall along the Pennsylvania Railroad's bed opposite Letchworth Park's Inspiration Point is a reminder of Johnson's ill-fated tunnel of the 1840s.

It's known as the "Bat Cave," because for six or seven months each year some 2,000 small brown bats hibernate in its bleak interior. Only scientists who come to study the bats are allowed by park rangers to enter the tunnel. A strong barrier keeps the public from visiting it. The danger of rock slides still exists and bats can be unfriendly toward intruders.

Part of the Johnson legend in the Genesee Country is the strange abode he built on a cliff above the tunnel. He named it Hornby Lodge after the Englishman who once owned the land. Johnson called the acreage around the lodge, "Tunnel Park."

The lodge was four stories high, built of logs and it contained 18 rooms. The ceiling of its eight-sided central room was supported by a huge oak with its bark left on and its roots exposed. A carpet was fitted around this sylvan pillar.

A winding stairway led to a fourth floor observatory, where a multitude of stuffed squirrels and birds perched. The lodge was full of rustic couches with hair mattresses for cushions.

In this extraordinary setting the imaginative canal

builder entertained lavishly. Sometimes there were 50 guests for dinner. It was at Hornby Lodge that a Johnson daughter, Mary, was married to George Mumford of Rochester. A blizzard marooned the whole company there for days.

The grandeur of the river chasm and the waterfalls enchanted Gov. William H. Seward and he commissioned a noted artist, Thomas Cole, to paint the scene. While Cole was at work, he lived at Hornby Lodge. His painting hangs in the Seward Mansion in Auburn.

In 1849 blasting for the canal made the lodge untenable and it was razed. By then Elisha Johnson was far from the Genesee Country. He had quit the canal enterprise in 1844.

About that time his son, Mortimer, killed a neighbor in a duel in the eastern part of the state and, facing a murder charge under New York law, he fled to Florida. In 1845 Mortimer turned up in the old hunting grounds of the Cherokee Indians along the Tellico in Tennessee.

At Tellico Plains a small iron furnace had been operating since 1824. Young Johnson saw possibilities in the Tellico Iron Co. and wrote about it to his father, then at loose ends for the first time in his busy life.

Elisha Johnson went to Tennessee and in 1846 with his son and his brother, Ebenezer, a former mayor of Buffalo, bought the iron works, enlarged the plant and purchased 30,000 neighboring acres of ore and timber.

Then he built the brick house on the banks of the Tellico River which in those parts is known as the Mansion. It stands near the log blockhouse which John Sevier, who created the short-lived independent State of Franklin, had built while fighting the Cherokees in 1788.

Elisha again displayed his penchant for unusual dwellings. He had the huge panes for his mansion's first floor windows hauled by wagon from Baltimore. His daughter, Mary, brought from France the heavy cornices of the living and dining rooms.

Johnson's wife, Betsey, appears in history only in an old deed recorded in Rochester. Naturally she was overshadowed by the powerful personality of her husband. Any wife of Elisha Johnson, short of a Catherine the Great or an Elizabeth, would have suffered the same fate.

Strangest of all the appurtenances of the big house on the Tellico were the three wooden ladders extending from the second floor. The neighbors did not believe they were intended for fire escapes but rather to provide a quick exit for Mortimer should New York law catch up with him.

For 18 years, from 1846 to 1864, the Johnsons lived in the Mansion. The iron works and a distillery they operated on the side prospered until the Civil War broke out. Then the Confederate government took over the plant for the making of ordnance and the Yankee Johnsons had to make munitions for the Rebel armies.

After the Union victory at Missionary Ridge in 1863, Gen. William Tecumseh Sherman sent several of his blue-clad divisions into eastern Tennessee. Before he began his march to the sea, Sherman and an aide visited Tellico Plains. They stayed two nights at the Mansion and the

Union general presided over a military trial in which the Johnsons were cleared of deliberate aid to the enemy.

It is said that Sherman was given a grand feast in the Mansion. Nevertheless that hard-bitten warrior ordered the iron foundry torn down lest it again serve the Confederacy. It never was rebuilt and some of the ruins still remain.

After the destruction of their iron works, the Johnsons left the Mansion and the South, never to return. They returned to New York State in 1864. The head of the clan, who had made and lost fortunes on both sides of the Mason-Dixon Line, died at the home of a daughter in Ithaca shortly after his return to the North. His wife had passed away in 1860 at Tellico Plains before the war and reverses came.

It is wild country down there in the old Cherokee Nation and a large tract around the Mansion has been taken over by the United States Forestry Service as a wild life refuge. Wild boars are among the game hunted in its woodlands. It is a sport stout old Elisha Johnson would have relished.

An old picture reveals a colorful, rugged personality. The man, with a leonine head crowned by a tall silk hat, the keen, indomitable eyes, the strong hands grasping a gold-headed cane, looks like a character out of Dickens.

Chapter 6

Call of the Thunder Water

The Indians did not regard the Falls of Niagara as a backdrop for death-defying stunts. They stood in humble reverence before one of nature's grandest masterpieces.

They heard the voices of their gods in the roar of the tumbling waters. They discerned mystical beings in the eternally rising mist. They brought the products of their fields and the trophies of the chase as tribute to the Spirit that dwelt in the "Thunder Water."

Then the conquering white men came and they, too, thrilled to the majesty of the scene. But they did not stand aside in worshipful awe. To them the mighty cataracts and the raging rapids spoke a challenge. "Here is something else to conquer."

The more practical of the white men harnessed the waters to create the magic electric power and exploited the scenic glories of Niagara Falls to bring in the tourists' dollars.

Venturesome and glory-seeking souls sought to conquer the Niagara in another way. Through the years they have been jumping off cliffs, riding barrels over the falls, swimming the mad whirlpool, walking tight ropes and cables at dizzy heights above the river chasm. The toll of the daredevils is a heavy one.

Exhibition promoters appeared on the scene as early as 1827.

Early that Autumn, handbills in bold type flooded the Niagara Frontier, announcing that on Sept. 8 "the pirate ship Michigan with a cargo of Furious Animals would sail through the tossing and deep rolling rapids of Niagara and down its Grand Precipice into the basin below."

The Michigan was an old schooner, condemned as unseaworthy, which had been bought by a little group for the stunt. The "furious animals" were a cow, a horse, a sheep and a bear. As the promoters advertised refreshments along with the show, a large crowd gathered on Goat Island where many tables had been set. Each diner was supposed to leave 50 cents for the meal.

The repast was nearly over when a shout went up: "The boat is coming." The crowd rushed to the bank to see the ship "go down the Grand Precipice." Most of them forgot to leave the 50 cents for the meal. The Michigan, with its cargo, reached the basin safely, but the bear had jumped off near the center of the rapids and set out for shore.

The promoters of that stunt had served the greatest free lunch in Niagara's history.

Sam Patch, whose specialty was leaping off high places into foaming waters, probably was the first daredevil to perform at the Falls.

On Oct. 7, 1829 Sam made a 70-foot leap from the lower end of Goat Island before a small turnout. He advertised a far greater spectacle for Oct. 17, a jump from a 120-foot platform on Goat Island. A large crowd saw him kiss the American flag as he leaped and emerged safely from the waters.

After that feat, Patch went to Rochester, where on Nov. 6 he successfully jumped into the Genesee at the high falls. On Friday, the 13th of November, he tried to repeat the stunt as 7,000 spectators watched. This time he did not emerge from the water. His body was found at Charlotte, near the mouth of the Genesee, the next year.

The year 1859 brought to Niagara Falls one of the ace exhibitionists of all time. He was a Frenchman, Jean Francois Gravelet. History knows him as Blondin. On a slender cable stretched across the river chasm he began a series of hair-raising stunts.

At dizzy heights above the racing waters, with his long balancing rod, he pranced, he walked backwards, he lay down, he performed on stilts and with baskets on his feet. He crossed the abyss with a sack on his head and body, leaving his arms and legs free. He pushed a wheelbarrow between two nations on his cable. He dropped a cord to the deck of the little steamer, the Maid of the Mist, far below him in midstream, pulled up a bottle and drank from it. His crowning exploit was carrying his manager across on his back. For three Summers he performed at the Falls and thrilled thousands, including a royal visitor, the Prince of Wales, who became King Edward VII.

After Blondin came a procession of daredevils, none of whom eclipsed the Frenchman's dizzy feats. The 1880s saw many attempts to negotiate the lower rapids in barrels and boats and by plain swimming.

A lean cooper, Carlisle Graham, made five trips through the rapids in a barrel. Maud Willard tried the trip in Graham's barrel and lost her life. William Potts and George Hazlett, Buffalonians, triumphed in a barrel. Hazlett repeated the stunt with his girl friend, Sadie Allen, beside him.

The only swimmer who conquered the full three miles of lower rapids was a big Boston cop, William Kendall, who made it in 1886 with the aid of a cork life belt. Capt. Matthew Webb, first victor over the English channel, tried in 1883 and lost. Several swimmers have negotiated the stretch below the Whirlpool. No one has tried it in recent years.

In 1889 Steve Brodie of Brooklyn Bridge fame jumped from a bridge into the Niagara River in a suit of India rubber, padded and reinforced by steel bands.

Lincoln Beachey's feat of flying a plane beneath the Rainbow bridge was considered sensational in 1911.

Until 1901 no one attempted to go over the Falls in a barrel. Nobody has ever been foolhardy enough to brave the American Falls with its tons of jagged rock. Four daredevils have made the plunge over the Horseshoe Falls and lived to tell the tale. Three others who tried lost their lives. One stunt was stopped by police.

Leading the procession was a 46-year-old widowed

schoolteacher from Michigan. Her name was Mrs. Anna Edson Taylor and she was a determined, if unglamorous, daredevil. She arrived at the Falls in October, 1901, with a crude, steel-bound oaken barrel, weighing some 260 pounds, including a 100 pound anvil strapped to the bottom for ballast.

On Oct. 24 rivermen strapped the buxom teacher in her barrel and towed it into the Niagara River. A quarter of a mile from the brink of the 161-foot cataract, the barrel was released. It landed in a deep and relatively calm pool after its plunge. It drifted toward the Canadian side, where rivermen opened it.

They found a soaking wet woman, suffering from mild shock and with a cut over an ear but very much alive. Anna Edson Taylor had made history. She was the first ever to go over the Falls.

She had won fame but fortune eluded her. She went on a poorly managed vaudeville tour. She told of her experience in a harsh voice and she lacked platform charm. Her managers should have insisted on her bringing her barrel with her. That might have saved her act.

When she went back after it, it had disintegrated. She had a second barrel made and in later life sat beside it in Falls Street in Niagara Falls, N.Y., autographing her pictures for tourists.

Anna Edson Taylor, a plucky pioneer, died in the Niagara County Infirmary at Lockport in 1921, a public charge. The county paid for her burial in Oakwood Cemetery, Niagara Falls, N.Y.

Ten years passed before another challenger appeared. He was Bobby Leach, a cocky little Englishman and circus stunt man, who made the plunge in a carefully constructed steel drum on July 25, 1911. He spent 23 weeks in a hospital with two broken knee caps and a shattered jaw. Unlike Mrs. Taylor, he made money, through tours and exhibiting his barrel. He also ran restaurants, which padded his bank account. Leach made two parachute jumps, one from a bridge and another from an airplane near the Falls, several years after his major exploit.

Bobby Leach, a daredevil all his life, slipped on a banana peel in a New Zealand street and suffered a broken leg in 1926. Gangrene set in and ironically, the second victor over Niagara died in bed.

Most foolhardy of the lot was Charles G. Stephens, a barber of Bristol, England, and the father of 11 children. In 1920 he went to his death in a crude wooden barrel with an anvil strapped to his feet. Only an arm, torn from its socket, and parts of his barrel were found.

In 1928 Jean Lussier entered the lists. A native of New Hampshire he had lived his boyhood in Quebec and when he returned to New England at the age of 16, he could speak no English—only French.

His first sight of Niagara Falls spawned his decision to conquer the cataract. But he wanted no part of any barrel for his ride. Instead he used a specially constructed rubber ball, nine feet in diameter. Lussier designed it, spending many months in Akron, Ohio, working on it.

Two layers of rubber and fabric were stretched over a

double steel frame. A 150-pound weight provided ballast. Tubes equipped with check bars and safety valves provided an entry for air and protection against water. Tanks filled with 40 hours supply of oxygen also went along.

As 150,000 persons watched, on July 4, 1928, the ball Jean had designed bounced neatly over the precipice and he was taken out, safe and sound, 50 minutes after the start of his journey.

Lussier went on tour for years, billed as the only man to have gone over the Falls and survived. Spry at 76, he now lives in a rooming house four blocks from the cataract he conquered.

The fate of the next challenger was not so happy. He was George L. Stratakis of Buffalo, a chef of Greek extraction, who rode to death on July 5, 1930, in a barrel of oak, bound by steel bands. It was caught behind the Falls and the 46-year-old chef suffocated. His mascot, a 100-year old turtle, survived. Stratakis had taken along a pad on which he said he would record his sensations during the trip. Not a mark had been made on the pad.

One of the best known rivermen was William (Red) Hill Sr., who before his death in 1942 from the effects of being gassed in World War I, had saved 28 lives and recovered 149 bodies from the Niagara. Three times he had gone through the lower rapids in a barrel.

With such a heritage, it is little wonder that his sons, William (Red) Jr. and Major Lloyd, should not only emulate their father in shooting the rapids, but also endeavor to conquer the 161-foot Horseshoe Falls.

The younger son, Major (that's his given name, not a military title), was first to make the try. On July 17, 1950 he crawled into a cigar-shaped stainless steel barrel. Before it reached the brink of the Falls, it struck a submerged wire mesh which spun it into shore. There Canadian police stepped in and stopped the stunt by pulling the irate Major Hill from his barrel.

Red Hill Jr. built an encased contraption of truck inner tubes, webbing and a fish net and on Aug. 5, 1951 made the plunge over the cataract. The angry waters smashed his vehicle, and Hill's body was found in Canadian waters the next day.

Ten years passed before another daredevil showed up. He was a personable young man who called himself "Nathan Boya" and told a fantastic story of a pledge made to his lady love in France to conquer Niagara Falls.

Whatever his motivation was, this newcomer designed a steel and rubber ball, patterned after the one Jean Lussier rode to glory in 1928. On July 15, 1961 he climbed into his ball which bobbed over the Falls and was picked up in the lower river by a Canadian launch. He escaped with cuts and bruises and a $113 fine for violating Dominion law.

"Boya's" real name was revealed as William Fitzgerald and he was a New York City maintenance man. What compulsion drove him to risk his life remains a mystery.

The police of two nations, who are maintaining a much closer watch around the cataract, believe he may have been the last of the daredevils to seek glory in conquering the Falls.

In this space age, the call of "the thunder water" has lost its glamor. Three persons lost their lives in their attempts and the four who survived found only fleeting fame and no great fortune.

the last of the Catholics to vote them to resume in the
1515.

In this passage, the author, who appeared wander by the
by-plane. Those readers had little faith in the associate
to take his argument had found new exciting has, and no
great interest.

Chapter 7

Seward's Finest Hour

Fate has not been kind to the memory of William Henry
Seward.

It is ironic that the statesman from Auburn is doomed to
wander down the path of history under the eternal shadow
of a man he considered intellectually his inferior and who
snatched from him the prize he most desperately wanted—
the Presidency of the United States.

Today William H. Seward is remembered only as Abraham Lincoln's Secretary of State. A few historians may
know about his cut-rate purchase of Alaska for Uncle Sam.
Once it was known as "Seward's Folly."

The brilliant and ambitious Auburn politician-lawyer
cast a massive shadow of his own in his lifetime. From
1831, when at the age of 30 he became a State Senator,
until his death in 1872, two years after he had completed
eight years' service as Secretary of State, he was constantly
in the public eye—and much of the time in public office.

He served two terms as Governor of New York and two
terms in the United States Senate, largely through the

44

tireless efforts of his political partner and crony, Thurlow Weed, the Whig boss of the Empire State. Seward was the leading anti-slavery Whig and after the Republican party was organized, he became its outstanding figure.

He was the "Mr. Republican" of 1860 and all signs (there were no polls in those days) pointed to his being the party's nominee for President that year. But he had been in public life too long, had taken too many stands, had made too many speeches and so many enemies that he was passed over for the more "available" and less vulnerable Lincoln of Illinois.

Lincoln had the benefit of the galleries his managers had packed with yelling Middle West partisans, for the second convention of the Grand Young Party was held in the newly built Wigwam in Chicago, Lincoln territory. "Old Abe" lived in Springfield, Ill.

His managers made deals, promised cabinet seats and generally outmaneuvered the Seward forces, although they were led by that master of the lobby, Thurlow Weed. So the cannon his fellow townsmen had hauled on the lawn of the Seward mansion at Auburn, ready to be fired when their hero, who stayed away from Chicago, was nominated, was never fired.

As Lincoln's prime minister, Seward at first tried to take over but found the ungainly prairie lawyer was not to be bossed. Seward saw the light and came to respect the President.

Of all the speeches Seward had made, two phrases from them have survived the years. In the great Senate debate of

1850 over the extension of slavery to newly admitted states, Seward rose to oppose compromise and declare that "there is a Higher Law than the Constitution." And in 1859, speaking in Rochester's old Corinthian Hall, Seward used the memorable words, "irrepressible conflict," in warning of the impending Civil War.

Seward had a ready flow of words and unlimited self-confidence. He was equally at ease with titled diplomats or backwoodsmen. He was slim, blue-eyed, sandy haired, with a beardless, sallow face and beetling eyebrows. His eagle beak of a nose was his most prominent feature. In a thoughtful mood, he would cock his head on one side, "like a wise macaw," as a contemporary put it.

He was studiously careless in his dress, forever spilling ashes from his cigar. He was a cultivated man but never stuffy. Although he traveled widely, he never wanted to live anywhere but in Auburn. His stately old mansion there has been recently converted into a Seward Museum.

"Bill" Seward was a successful lawyer, formidable in the court room and wise in all the tricks of his profession. In politics he was a realist. He could shift position or sidestep an issue with the dexterity of an acrobat. He was a business-minded public official, conservative in fiscal matters.

Thus emerges a picture of an adroit politician, a foxy lawyer, a smart manipulator. That is oversimplification and not the whole picture. Seward's was a complex personality. There was an idealistic streak in his makeup. At times he was impulsive. His nature was basically warm under the politician's mask.

Many times in his career he demonstrated his sympathy for the underdog. He was a sincere enemy of slavery. As governor, he championed the cause of the immigrants crowding into New York and other cities, and of the Anti-Renters in their revolt against the feudal patroons of Eastern New York.

The cynics might say these acts were tinged with politics. There was no politics in what might be called Seward's finest hour. It was in 1846 and he was practicing law in Auburn, in a lull in his office holding between the governor's chair and a seat in the Senate. At that time the compassionate, humanitarian side of his nature was clearly revealed.

Without any hope of material reward and at risk of bodily harm to himself, as well at great cost to his local prestige and popularity, the former Governor gave many months of his time, energy and his talents to saving from the gallows a poor, demented Negro slayer—while the whole countryside was demanding the prisoner's life.

Seward's client was William Freeman, born in Cayuga County in 1824 of a Negro father who had been reared in slavery and of a half Indian, half Negro mother. His Indian blood gave him a roaming instinct and he did not stay long on a job. He resented any restraint. But generally he was a youth of average intelligence and normal personality until he was 16 years old.

At that time he was falsely accused of stealing a horse and was sent to Auburn Prison for five years on the testimony of the man who later turned out to be the real thief.

The injustice of the sentence rankled within Freeman. In prison he protested his innocence repeatedly. He was often disciplined. During one flogging Freeman fought back and the guard struck the Negro youth a brutal blow over the head with a board.

That blow made him permanently deaf, caused brain damage and altered his whole personality. He became dull, brooding, incoherent, childlike, given to sudden fits of rage. This was the William Freeman turned loose on society in September, 1845.

After his release he worked at odd jobs in and around Auburn. He babbled incessantly of the five years he had been imprisoned for a crime he did not commit, of his being beaten by the guard and he would say over and over: "They must pay for it." He did not specify who "they" were but twice he went to a magistrate seeking warrants for "the folks who sent him to prison."

The early months of 1846 found Freeman boarding with a Negro washerwoman in what was called New Guinea, one mile south of Auburn. He paid for his keep by carrying baskets of clothes to and from the village.

Two miles farther south, in the Town of Fleming on the west shore of Owasco Lake in a frame house lived a prosperous and respected farmer, John G. Van Nest. He was of Dutch descent. In his household were his wife, Sarah; her mother, Mrs. Phebe Wyckoff, a daughter and two sons, the youngest not quite two years old.

There is no evidence that Willie Freeman had ever

48

known the Van Nests or that any of them had been involved in sending him to prison.

Owasco Lake was bathed in moonlight when at 9:30 on the night of March 12, 1846, a young Negro, with a butcher knife in his hand and senseless murder in his mind, approached the Van Nest farmhouse. He found Mrs. Van Nest standing in the back yard and without warning, he plunged the knife into her breast. Fatally wounded, she managed to stagger, screaming, into the house.

Her husband from the living room heard her cry and ran toward the door. The maniac met him there and stabbed Van Nest to death before the farmer could resist. The mad butchery went on. The 70-year-old Mrs. Wyckoff, a widow, was stabbed twice. She fought back valiantly and in the struggle wounded her attacker on the wrist with a kitchen knife. Then the infant Van Nest son was stabbed to death in his bed.

The others in the house fled to safety, all but a guest for the night, Cornelius Van Arsdale. When the Negro came upstairs, Van Arsdale tussled with him and although he was wounded, he threw a candlestick at the intruder, sending the slayer tumbling down the stairs. Van Arsdale grabbed a broomstick and drove the Negro from the kitchen and out into the night.

Before he left the Van Nest property, he stole a horse from the barn and galloped away in the moonlight. After the fashion of modern gangsters who flee in a series of stolen cars, this desperado abandoned the Van Nest horse and stole another in his flight.

The next morning William Freeman, a suspect from the description given by Van Arsdale, was picked up in Oswego County, 30 miles from the Van Nest farmhouse. He admitted his guilt with indifference and laughed at his captors when he was asked why he had killed the Van Nests. Brought back in chains to the scene of his crime, he faced a magistrate in the Van Nest home and was charged with murder.

A belligerent crowd gathered. The Van Nests had been popular and the cold blooded killings aroused the countryside. The crowd's wrath ran higher with word that Mrs. Wyckoff had died, bringing the killer's score to four. There were cries of "lynch him" and "kill the black ape now." The Cayuga County sheriff and his men had difficulty getting Freeman back safely into the jail at Auburn.

Three days later four coffins were carried out of the old brick Reformed Protestant Dutch Church at the crossroads near the foot of Owasco Lake. The four victims of a madman were buried in the little Sand Beach cemetery with so many Dutch names on its headstones.

A long, low stone, with lilies of the valley at its base, today marks the burial place of the three Van Nests. These words are engraved upon their tomb: "All murdered on March 12, 1846." Nearby is the grave and headstone for the fourth victim.

The funeral attracted another tense and sullen crowd. Its ugly mood was inflamed by the minister's sermon which closed with this solemn injunction:

"I appeal to this vast assembly to maintain the laws of

this country inviolate and cause the murderer to be punished."

Copies of that sermon were widely distributed. The newspapers played up the gory crime and its aftermath, and interest in the case spread beyond Auburn and Cayuga County. The Auburn jail was well guarded, for there were those who would have strung up Freeman to the nearest tree without any legal formalities.

Such was the situation when a few days after the crime, "Governor" Seward, as he was still known in Auburn, came home from a business trip to Albany.

At the time Seward had an appeal pending from the conviction of Henry Wyatt, an Auburn convict who had slain a fellow prisoner in 1845. The noted lawyer had been moved by the sight of Wyatt manacled to the prison floor and believing the man to be mentally irresponsible, had volunteered to defend him through a plea of insanity.

Friends warned Seward not to intervene in the Freeman case. They told him of the temper of the public and urged him not to jeopardize his political future. Seward listened and kept his own counsel.

He visited Freeman in his cell. He found him unable to carry on a coherent conversation. Seward's sense of justice was outraged that one so obviously unbalanced should be railroaded to the gallows.

The former Governor demanded a jury trial of Freeman's sanity. In his view, should the young Negro be found insane, he should be committed to an asylum for the rest of his life. If found sane, he should be tried.

Seward's course was a most unpopular one. Hotheads warned him if there was a delay in the execution of the slayer of four innocent people, an enraged public would take matters into its own hands. He was told it did not matter whether or not the killer was insane. He should hang as a warning to potential murderers.

On a return from a trip, Seward was met at the railroad station by friends who came to warn and protect him. A mob gathered before the Seward mansion and hurled some ugly threats before it dispersed. Taunts and threats from a hostile crowd for the first time in his life greeted the former Governor of New York as he walked the streets of Auburn.

The lawyer "kept his cool," to use a modern phrase. He fought for two hectic weeks to have his client declared insane. He produced a long list of witnesses, including several physicians, in his battle to convince the jury. Willie Freeman bolstered his own case by his vacant stare and general air of indifference to the proceedings.

William Seward lost his fight. A lone juror who stood against a sanity verdict was privately lectured by the presiding judge. That juror yielded to the extent that he joined in a verdict which declared "the prisoner sufficiently sane in mind and memory to determine right from wrong."

So the trial of William Freeman for murder was moved for immediate action despite Seward's demand for delay. When the Negro faced the court and was asked by the district attorney if he had counsel, the prisoner mumbled "I don't know."

Then the former Governor rose, pale, but with determination in his hollow voice, to announce:

"May it please the court, I shall remain counsel for the prisoner until his death."

Throughout July of 1846 the battle went on in the Auburn court house. Before a crowd openly hostile, Seward fought with skill every step of the way. He made the sanity of the defendant the sole issue and both sides called many witnesses, medical and lay.

At the close of the trial Seward's summation was a lengthy, careful and masterful review of the evidence. It also contained the most heartfelt utterances of his career. His peroration, in that curious husky voice that was to be heard in national debate, went:

"I plead not for a murderer. I have no inducement, no motive to do so. I have addressed my fellow citizens in many various relations when reward of fame or wealth awaited me. I have been cheered by manifestations of popular approbation and sympathy and when there was no such encouragement, I had at least the gratitude of those whose cause I had defended.

"I speak now in the hearing of people prejudiced against this prisoner and who condemn me for speaking in his behalf.

"He is a convict, a pauper, a Negro, without intellect, sense or emotion, I am not the prisoner's lawyer. I am indeed a volunteer in his behalf but society and mankind have the deepest interests. I am the lawyer for society and for mankind, shocked beyond the power of expression at the scene I have witnessed here, of trying a maniac as a malefactor. There is not a white man or white woman who would not have been dismissed long ago from the peril of such prosecution."

Attorney General John Van Buren, son of a former President, answered with the effective argument that "the peace of the community is the sole issue here and if a crime of this magnitude is to go unpunished and thus to invite imitation, it is your hearth stones that will be drenched in blood."

The verdict was guilty. Seward had lost again. William Freeman, who could not even comprehend the words of the sentence, was doomed to the gallows on Sept. 18.

Still Seward fought on. He appealed the verdict to the higher court and won a new trial. Before a second trial could be held, William Freeman was called before a higher tribunal. They found the Negro dead in his cell on August 21, 1847.

After it was all over, Seward wrote these words, which are in his autobiography:

"Perhaps years hence when the passion and excitement which agitate this community shall have passed away, some wandering stranger, some lone exile . . . may erect over my remains a humble stone and thereupon put this epitaph. 'HE WAS FAITHFUL.' "

In a shady dell of Auburn's Fort Hill cemetery is a plain

3. Elisha Johnson, Pioneer Promoter

4. Johnson Canal Tunnel, Now "Bat Cave"

tablet-like stone. On its front is inscribed: "William H. Seward, born May 16, 1801. Died October 10, 1872."

In the rear of the stone on the base of a short ornamental urn are these words:

"HE WAS FAITHFUL."

Chapter 8

"Sha-lot"

When Mark Twain visited Rochester on a lecture tour years ago, seemingly the only impression of the city that lingered with the gangling humorist was the fact that "it has a neighboring village named Charlotte, but which the natives pronounce 'Sha-lot.' "

Other visitors and newcomers to Rochester still are aghast at the curious local corruption of a woman's given name when applied to a community.

Actually there is no Charlotte today. You won't find the name on any official map. In 1916 the lakeside village in the Town of Greece was gobbled up by the expanding city and it became the 23d Ward of Rochester.

Area residents still call by the old name the place where the Genesee River, after coursing northward 130 miles from a little spring in the Pennsylvania mountains, joins the waters of Lake Ontario. Nothing will ever change that misplaced accent on the second syllable, although the "r" in Charlotte, as pronounced locally, is not completely silent, as Twain would have us believe.

Charlotte is older than Rochester. Her first settlers came in the 18th Century when Western New York was a wilderness. It was a Great Lake port and had a customs house when Rochester was a swamp.

Had it not been for the waterfalls that powered the mills and the advent of the Erie Canal, the principal city of the Genesee Country might well today be at the lakeside, and not eight miles to the southward where Nathaniel Rochester laid out his first village lots in 1811.

In its long lifetime Charlotte has been many things—a lake port where the masts of the sailing ships towered thick in the early time and Charlotte-built schooners plied the Great Lakes—a key outpost during the War of 1812, threatened by British invasion—a pleasant village with a growing summer colony and a busy waterfront, for always there was the trade with Canada across the lake—then the gaudy years when Ontario Beach Park was "The Coney Island of the West," with its big hotels, its teeming midway and its long excursion trains.

Today it still is a playground, of a sort. There is a large and modern bath house and a fine sandy beach in a city park dotted with picnic benches and shelters. But as this is written, it appears there will be no host of merry bathers in Lake Ontario this year, maybe not for many Summers, Algae, the sea weed, which "killed" its sister lake, Erie, has infested Ontario to an alarming extent. Also the waters of the Genesee empty a mass of pollution into the lake.

The lakeside park still draws its sun bathers and picnickers, but the pollution problem is writing a dark chapter in a story of gayety.

Only graybeards remember the amusement park in its heyday, with the thrills of its Virginia Reel and Scenic Railway, its animal acts, chant of the barkers, all the noise and color of a mad and merry midway.

Gone are the days of the excursion steamboats, the shoe box picnic lunches, the bicyclists and the cinder paths, the Gibson Girl with leg of mutton sleeves, parasol and pompadour; the gay blade with buttoned shoes and derby hat; of the two-piece bathing suits with the high neck and long stockings; of the surrey with the fringe on top, when mandolins tinkled in the moonlight and young voices blended in "The Good Old Summertime" and in "The Shade of the Old Apple Tree," those tranquil days before the horseless carriage came to change our whole way of life.

Not that "Sha-lot" today is any deserted village. Despite the ban on bathing, it is a refuge for heat-plagued city dwellers. The 23d is a populous ward and its citizens believe there is no better place to live the year around than at the lakeside.

Charlotte's more colorful years belong to the past.

The big hotels are gone and the long excursion trains no longer rumble into Ontario Beach Park. River Street, where once the sailors roistered and the business places were centered, is quiet now.

The cry, "To the merry-go-round," which was a battle call like the "Hey, Rube" of a circus, is heard no more and there are no gang fights at the carousel. Even the car ferries and the steamboats which for so many years linked Charlotte with Cobourg, Kingston, Toronto and other Canadian ports, no longer ply the big lake.

One picturesque relic of the long ago still stands, a lonely sentinel, on the hill near the river's mouth. It is the stone lighthouse which was built in 1822. Not since 1883 has "The Upper Light" thrown its friendly beams to guide mariners on the lake. Each year the creeping vines weave a thicker blanket over the staunch old landmark.

The old lighthouse stands on historic ground. It was there in 1791 that Charlotte's first settler, William Hincher, a soldier of the Revolution and a fugitive from Shay's "army" of rebellious small farmers against the commonwealth of Massachusetts, built a log shanty, with the help of his 11-year-old son and roofed it with wild grass the two had cut. Then they returned to Massachusetts.

The next February, the Hinchers, man and wife, the son and seven daughters, came through the drifted wilds, along blazed trails in the woods, to their new home. The Hinchers were the first white family to live on the lakeshore between Oswego and Niagara.

Other pioneers, mostly from New England, came and founded a village at the river's mouth. In 1805 the Port of the Genesee was established and Samuel Latta, the first customs agent, built a warehouse at the foot of the street which bears his name. Town lots were laid out and a store, a wharf and a cluster of houses were built.

The settlers visioned a lakeport city and for a time their

dream seemed likely to come true. For a thriving commerce was developed with Canada and schooners, some of them built at Charlotte, carried wheat, whiskey, potash, pork and other products of the York State frontier across the lake.

One mariner, who in 1807 built the first hotel at Charlotte, lives in lakeside folklore—because of his many voyages on the sea of matrimony. His name was Samuel Currier and he won and lost seven wives. Six of them died, four in three years. It is said he buried three in one grave. Seemingly all the deaths were natural. The seventh deserted Sam. In 1823 Currier's body was found in the river below the Lower Falls. He had removed his clothes, hung them on a bush and leaped in the cataract to join his many wives in death.

In 1811 a deed was recorded which for the first time contained the words, "Village of Charlotte." There are several versions of the origin of the name.

One is that it was called after Charlotte Augusta, daughter of King George IV of England, although it hardly seems probable that people who had so recently won their independence from Britain, would so honor a member of the royal house.

Another is that the village was named for Charlotte, the daughter of Robert Troup, agent for the British Pulteney interests that once owned the site of the village.

The third version is that the name honors Charlotte, the wife of Sir John Lowther Johnstone, one of the Pulteney heirs whose name appeared on early deeds. Certainly it was named after a woman—who did not pronounce her name "Sha-lot."

Panic spread along the thinly settled lakeside during the War of 1812 when the British landed at Charlotte in June, 1813, and unmolested, seized salt, whiskey and other provisions from the village store. In September of that year the rival fleets fought an indecisive three-hour engagement in the lake several miles off Charlotte. The enemy withdrew with the heavier losses.

The British came again, on the night of May 14, 1814, with a fleet of 13 sail under the "hit and run" commodore, Sir James Yeo. Invasion seemed certain. The rest is a favorite Rochester tale—how 33 members of a militia outfit, Stone's Dragoons, all the able bodied men of Rochesterville, marched down to the river's mouth in the rainy night and at dawn marched and countermarched among the trees on shore to bluff the British into the belief they faced a formidable defense force.

As the story goes, a British officer came ashore under a flag of truce to tell the settlers that if they would surrender their stores, the fleet would sail away without firing a single shot. Whereupon Francis Brown, miller and a captain of Dragoons, in reply thundered, "Blood knee deep first!"

Meanwhile reinforcements from the interior joined the defenders, and the enemy, after a desultory and harmless exchange of cannon balls, sailed off, never to return to Charlotte.

After the War of 1812, commerce was revived with

Canada. With the completion of the Erie Canal in 1825, Rochester grew into a roaring boom town, the nation's foremost milling center, dwarfing the lake port. But Charlotte shared in the boom with heavy shipments of flour to Canadian ports.

Also shipped across the lake before the Civil War were some pitiful human cargoes. Many a fugitive Negro slave was spirited aboard ships at Charlotte, bound for Canada and freedom in the days of the Underground Railway.

During the Civil War the lakeside got the invasion jitters. In 1864 just before the Presidential election wild rumors of a Confederate raid from Canada were spread and two field guns were mounted on the shore at Charlotte. The scare soon faded away.

At war's end, Marty McEntire's pier saloon which had catered largely to lake sailors, began to attract more genteel patrons as lake bathing became popular. McEntire provided dressing tents in front of his place and rented out bathing suits, discreet ones that covered most of the human frame. That was the birth of Charlotte as a summer resort.

In the 1870s the first Summer colony, a few families living mostly in tents, sprang up at the beach. Later some elegant Summer homes were built and Beach Avenue under its spreading trees became a "little Newport."

Side-wheeler excursion boats ran down the river from the Glen House at the Lower Falls. Rochesterians began coming down to the lake in the river boats, in their carriages and in Winter there were jolly sleighing parties to the new hotels built at Charlotte.

Then came the gaudy "Coney Island" chapter in the Charlotte story. It began in 1882 when the New York Central Railroad, which in 1853 had built a steam line from Rochester, bought a strip along the beach and river and leased it to private promoters for an amusement park.

A big hotel, the Ontario, was built. Grounds were laid out with wide boardwalk promenades, lawns and flower gardens. A brewery built the Bartholomay Pavilion, a huge beer garden featuring shore dinners and music. Then came a skating rink, shooting galleries, sausage stands, a chute which projected bathers into the surf, riding devices, a band stand, vaudeville acts and all the trappings of an amusement park.

Ontario Beach Park had its grand opening on Aug. 2, 1884. Excursion trains from all over Upstate New York and Northern Pennsylvania rolled over the loop in the park. Steamboats brought excursionists from Canada.

In 1889 an electric railway was completed from the Rochester city line to Charlotte. It went after its share of the excursion trade. But the railroad, which owned the amusement park, had the edge. Its trains ran right into "Coney Island." So it built a high fence around the park and charged an admission fee, which was included in the railroad fare. Those who came by trolley had to pay the admission charge in addition to their fare.

It is fitting that Sam Patch, the leaper of cataracts and the ace daredevil of his time, should be buried in Charlotte.

On St. Patrick's Day of 1830, a Charlotte farmer, breaking the river ice to water his horse, came upon the body of the young exhibitionist who on Nov. 13, 1829, in the sight of 7,000 horrified spectators, had leaped to his death at the Genesee Upper Falls.

Sam Patch was a homeless wanderer so they buried him in the cemetery along River Street with the pioneers. Not far from his last resting place, in later years many another daredevil was to thrill crowds at Ontario Beach Park, the miniature Coney Island.

Well in the van of that long death-defying procession was the younger Blondin, who in 1885 walked a high tight rope. One of his stunts was walking out on the rope, carrying a small oil stove, a table, a chair, a frying pan and an egg. In the middle of the rope, high above the crowd, he fried his egg, sat down and ate it.

In 1892 a distinguished guest visited the park. He did not fry an egg on a tight rope. He was a dignified, bearded, stocky man in a frock coat and he was Benjamin Harrison, President of the United States. When he came to Rochester to dedicate the Soldiers and Sailors Monument in Washington Square on Memorial Day, he and other notables had breakfast at Charlotte's Cottage Hotel. The Presidential party rode down to the lake and back in the street car company's "Palace Car," escorted by a parade of wheelmen.

In 1891 50,000 saw A. Leo Stevens, aged 16, and billed as the "Boy Daredevil of the Sky," begin his long career in aeronautics at Charlotte, where he parachuted from a balloon. Strong winds bore him out 18 miles on Lake

Ontario, where he spent a miserable three hours before the row boats of the Life Saving Crew reached him.

That "boy daredevil" later was to design the parachute pack and the first motor-driven dirigible. He pioneered in using a wireless receiving set in an airship. He made daring jumps all over the country and was a Signal Corps instructor in ballooning in World War I. Stevens died in 1945 in the midst of work on a revolutionary new parachute.

Nick Kaufman, the home town high-wheel trick bicyclist, who later performed all over the United States and in Europe, got his start at the amusement park in 1895.

Circuses, including Ringling Bros., pitched their tents on the beach. When the Bostock Animal Shows played at Ontario Beach, an added attraction was a wedding in a lion's cage. Vaudeville acts, name bands, summer opera all had their day at the amusement center.

In 1899 a lanky, obscure cowboy vaudevillian tried his rope tricks and drawling patter on an Ontario Beach crowd. It was a flop. He quit after one performance. His name was Will Rogers.

About that time Rochester's celebrated "Rattlesnake Pete" Gruber, operator of a curious museum-saloon, reptile expert and born showman, tried out in the river between the piers a nautical bicycle of his own invention. It was supposed to be propelled through the water by a paddle wheel. But the waves tossed it about so violently and the strong river current made the going so slow that Pete gave up the idea.

It has nothing to do with the amusement park but also in the 1890s, another inventor, John F. Cooney of Charlotte, tinkered with a rocket-propelled airplane. He was unable to raise funds to complete his invention. His neighbors laughed at him. But he did manage to construct a fuselage-covered plane, which he vainly attempted to drive with an oil-burning flame projector. John Cooney was a few years ahead of his time.

Some of the excursion trains brought some pretty tough customers to Charlotte. A trainload of Scranton coal miners once waged a gang melee with local talent that the police had to rush down from Rochester to quell. And whenever the "Sullivan Excursion" rolled in from Syracuse with its traveling bar, ten extra cops were detailed to the park and the village lockup was likely to be filled when night fell.

As the 20th Century romped into its second decade and the honk of the horseless carriage began to sound in the land, the star of Western New York's Coney Island dimmed. Steamboat passengers were fewer. Excursion trains were shorter. People were taking to the open road and far off places in their Model Ts, Moons and Marmons.

When in 1916 the village of Charlotte was annexed to the city of Rochester, which announced plans to establish a city park and bathing beach, it sounded the knell of the old amusement center.

The curtain fell with the end of the 1919 season. Mack Sennett's "California Bathing Beauties" was the farewell attraction. The fence and most of the buildings were torn down. The tracks of the loop were ripped up, along with the boardwalk. The big Ontario Hotel lingered on the scene until 1927.

Once many hotels lined River Street. The Steamboat House was the last to go. And the last of the oldtime hotel men, Sam Leary, who ran it for more than four decades, has passed away. Sam could tell many a tale of River Street in its hell roaring days, when the boats were so thick in the river opposite his place that one could walk across to the Summerville side on their decks.

Sam recalled when sailors, full of fight and grog, would drag their coats in the muddy streets, daring all and sundry to step on them. If any accepted the challenge, the battle was on. It was on the tradition of the old Irish war cry, "Tread on the Tail of Me Coat." Leary more than once looked from his windows across to the Rome, Watertown & Ogdensburg (Hojack) station to see three fights going on at once.

River Street is quiet now. No longer does the Hojack line bring carloads of fruit pickers from the orchard country after the harvest. It carries only freight and precious little of that. The road, a Penn Central branch, got its curious nickname, it is said, because a farmer, to quiet his mule, frightened by the Iron Horse, kept yelling: "Ho, Jack. Ho, Jack."

The old color-splashed Charlotte is gone. Only the memories linger in gray heads—memories of Jerry Flynn's where one could buy a helping of perch, chowder and a schooner of beer, all for 15 cents; of Gus Frank and his "hot" stand beside the river and under the Scenic Railway; of the Switchback and the canals of Venice; of the Wishing Cars, built for two, with a red heart painted on each white side; of the House of Mirth.

They are gone, with the steamboats that ran to Sea Breeze and the "ferry" Windsor, which plied the narrow water between Charlotte and Summerville before the jack-knife bridge was built over the Genesee. Gone, with the big hotels and the little joints, gone with the barkers, the bands, the trapeze performers and all the other remembered things that Grandpa and Grandma knew—when they were young and held hands under the trees in old Charlotte.

* * *

Out of the city's acquisition of the former amusement center as a public bathing beach and park emerged a fantastic legal struggle in which documents of 1786 were cited and which was carried up to the United States Supreme Court.

After 136 years the Commonwealth of Massachusetts laid claim to a strip of beach which was ceded to New York State by the Hartford Convention of 1786, which settled conflicting claims arising after the Revolution and rooted in grants of the Stuart kings of England to their colonies.

The agreement defined "the southern shore of Lake Ontario" as the boundary of the territory over which New York was granted sovereignty and Massachusetts the right to sell. The Bay State sold the tract pronto to land speculators in 1791—and that presumably ended the matter.

In 1922, Rochester officials, in the course of routine proceedings to acquire a clear title to the beach, raised the question. Massachusetts at once claimed the land, on the grounds that when it sold the tract in 1791, it was under water. Since the park was later formed from the lake by the drifting in of sand through the years, the Bay State contended it owned Ontario Beach because it lay north of the ancient shore line.

Finally in 1926, "the Nine Old Men" of the highest court threw out the Massachusetts claim, ruling that the title extended to the water's edge, regardless of any change in the shore line in 136 years.

So today bathers sunning themselves on the sands of Ontario Beach are not in a little bit of Massachusetts, with the New York State line a few yards away where their cars are parked.

Had the judges decided in favor of the Bay State, would the thrifty Yankees have charged tolls to the beach?

Sounds fantastic but anything can happen in old "Shalot."

Chapter 9

Fiend of the Finger Lakes

It was with good reason that Edward Rulloff was called "The Fiend of the Finger Lakes."

He did not look the arch criminal he was and he fooled a lot of people. He was a scholarly appearing man with a powerful frame and delicate womanish hands, along with ingratiating manners and a gentle, musical voice. His inscrutable face was framed in burnsides and chin whiskers and his massive head was tilted a little to one side like that of an expectant bird.

He might have been taken for a college professor, a doctor, even a minister. During his bizarre lifetime he posed at various times as each.

But the musical voice could on occasion pour out a torrent of profanity and filth; the delicate hands could deal out death and the dark gray eyes which seemed so guileless could blaze with murderous hate.

At heart Rulloff was a bandit and a murderer. Just how many he killed will never be known for a certainty. Suspicion was directed against him in the deaths of at least seven persons. But when he went to the gallows, it was for the fatal shooting of a clerk during the bungled holdup of a Binghamton store in 1870.

He was a crafty, slippery rogue who covered his tracks well—until his last job—and he talked himself out of many a desperate corner and slid out of many a jail.

Edward Rulloff's fantastic story is preserved in old records in Ithaca and at Cornell University, in newspaper files and in the folklore handed down through the generations.

His massive brain is preserved in alcohol at Stimson Hall at Cornell, with the other jars which hold the once famous collection started long ago by Dr. Burt Green Wilder. The Rulloff brain is heavier than the average. However, modern scientists hold that the size or weight of a human brain does not denote a corresponding mental capacity. Rulloff's skull was thicker than the average. So was his hide.

In the quarters of the De Witt Historical Society in downtown Ithaca, the old Courthouse built on the site of the one in which Rulloff first stood trial, there are on exhibit other mementoes of the villain of the Lakes Country.

There is a section of the heavy hand-wrought log chain, which according to tradition, shackled Rulloff in a basement cell of the old Clinton House. Under glass is a plaster cast of the murderer's features, made by an Ithaca artist and beside it is the broadside of 1859 when an enraged populace demanded Lynch Law justice for Edward Rulloff.

He was born Edward H. Rulloffson in St. John's, New Brunswick, in 1821 of respectable German stock. He was hardly out of his teens before he was in a Canadian jail after two mysterious fires in the store where he clerked coincided with two lootings of the stock.

In 1842 he drifted into Tompkins County on a canal boat. Soon he was teaching a "select school" in Dryden. Among his pupils was pretty 19-year-old Harriet Schutt, daughter of a farmer.

Harriet married the glib stranger on the last day of the year 1843. For a time they lived in a boarding house in Ithaca where Rulloff was employed by a botanical druggist from whom he picked up a smattering of medical lore. He had cards printed with "Doct. Edward H. Rulloff" on them. A few of them are preserved by the historical society in Ithaca.

According to testimony in his second trial, he was called to the home of his wife's brother, William H. Schutt, to treat a baby who appeared to have the colic. The child died in convulsions. Two days later the mother died suddenly. There were symptoms of poisoning and in later years, suspicion fell on Rulloff. There were no formal charges, just neighborhood talk.

After living for a time with Harriet's parents, the young couple moved around 1844 to a farmhouse at Lansing, five miles north of Ithaca and one and one half miles from Cayuga Lake.

Harriet and her three-months-old daughter were last seen alive on the late afternoon of June 23, 1845. Olive

Robertson, who lived with her parents across the road, later testified that mother and child appeared to be in good health.

The next morning Mrs. Thomas Robertson, mother of Olive, noticed that the shutters of the Rulloff house were closed, an unusual circumstance.

At noon that day Rulloff came to Robertson, asking the loan of a horse and wagon. He said he was returning a chest to one of the Schutt relatives who lived eight miles away. Later that relative swore he had never left any chest at Rulloff's and none was ever delivered to him.

Tom Robertson was to testify that after Rulloff "took dinner with us," his son drove the horse and wagon to their neighbor's house; that he saw the "doctor" pushing a chest toward the door. Robertson said he helped load it into the wagon and that "his end weighed 60 or 70 pounds." He said Rulloff came out with a sack which seemed to be about one third full and put it in the wagon; that the contents of chest or sack were never revealed and that Rulloff returned the horse and wagon about noon the next day.

Not until later did Robertson surmise what became almost universal belief in the region—that the heavy wooden box he had helped lift into his own wagon contained the bodies of Harriet Rulloff and baby.

Rulloff shortly left on the stage for Geneva, saying he was going West. He told Mrs. Robertson his wife had gone to visit in Madison, Ohio, and that she might be back "in two or three weeks, maybe never."

Court testimony by Harriet's relatives later revealed that the Rulloffs' married life was sometimes troubled and that the husband had exhibited a fierce jealousy of the attentions paid his wife by her cousin, young Doctor Bull.

In the testimony also is an account of Rulloff striking his wife with an iron pestle when she failed to grind some pepper fine enough to suit him. There also is a hearsay story of the husband trying to get his wife to take poison in a suicide pact. He was to drink the poison last.

In a few weeks after his "Western trip," Rulloff, with his usual aplomb, was back in the Ithaca area. In the meantime neighbors had found his wife's clothing scattered around the deserted house and ugly rumors were afloat. Rulloff expressed pained surprise.

He presumably was in flight when Harriet's brother, Ephraim Schutt, spotted him on the back platform of a westbound train in the Rochester station. Rulloff promised to accompany his brother-in-law to the Ohio village where he said his wife was staying. Rulloff gave Ephraim the slip on the docks at Buffalo. Schutt went to Madison, Ohio, where nobody had heard of his sister. By chance, on the return trip, he ran into Rulloff in Cleveland. He beckoned to a policeman and Edward Rulloff returned to Ithaca in irons.

Feeling ran high against him in Tompkins County but there was no clear evidence of murder. Cayuga Lake had been dragged but the search failed to turn up the chest many believed contained the bodies of mother and child.

So Rulloff was indicted and convicted on the lesser

charge of abducting his wife. He was sentenced to 10 years in Auburn Prison. During his confinement, he made so thorough a study of languages that in later years he was offered a professorship of a college, lectured as a learned philologist before a national scientific convention and claimed to have discovered a new universal language.

But on his release from Auburn, he was rearrested, this time on the charge of murdering his wife. He claimed double jeopardy and obtained a writ of habeas corpus. A new Grand Jury indicted him for the slaying of the child.

A long and historic legal battle ensued. Rulloff first obtained a change of venue to Tioga County but was convicted after trial in Owego and in October, 1856, was sentenced to be hanged. His attorneys, Boardman and Finch of Ithaca, appealed to the Appellate Division, which affirmed the conviction.

The jig seemed to be up for Edward Rulloff. But one of his lawyers was the resourceful and determined young Francis Miles Finch, then on the threshold of a distinguished career. Rulloff and Finch, several years his junior, had been the only members of a Greek class in the Ithaca Academy. Finch had no special affection for his former classmate but he was an able lawyer and prepared to carry the appeal to the state's highest tribunal, the Court of Appeals.

While his lawyer was mapping his strategy, the slippery Rulloff made the first of several jail breaks.

On a May night in 1857 a team of black horses wheeled a carriage to the outer door of the old stone jail in Ithaca.

A man sprang out of the shadows and leaped into the driver's seat. Through the night the carriage dashed over the hills, to Newfield and beyond. Horses and rig were found along the road the next day. Nobody ever claimed them.

The magnetic criminal had won over the young son of the Ithaca jailer. It was Albert Jarvis who left the door of the prisoner's cell unlocked. In later years Jarvis became Rulloff's accomplice and their last job together cost both of them their lives.

After his escape Rulloff showed up in Western Pennsylvania where the learning he had picked up in prison so impressed the head of a small college that he was offered a professorship. He chose to rob a jewelry store and was fleeing on foot with his loot when a man came along and offered him a ride in his buggy. It turned out that the horse had been stolen and the law caught up with its driver. Whereupon Rulloff characteristically repaid his benefactor by tossing the loot-laden bag into the back of the buggy and asserting it belonged to the horse thief.

Within a few months he was on his way back to Ithaca, again a prisoner. A hostler who had been a fellow convict at Auburn recognized Rulloff and turned him in.

In the meantime Finch had argued Rulloff's case before the State Court of Appeals at Albany and raised points that brought about a new judicial interpretation of the corpus delicti, "the body of the crime," not the physical body of a victim of murder but the essential element of the alleged crime.

He argued that the prosecution, in place of a corpus delicti, had put in the bare fact of disappearance. Finch won his appeal. The high court ruled that the circumstances were not so unequivocal and certain as to establish the fact and that the trial judge had erred in not discharging the prisoner at the conclusion of the evidence.

It was a smashing victory for the Ithaca lawyer who, carrying his first murder case to the state's highest tribunal, had raised the question of whether a person convicted of murder could be punished when there was no corpus delicti. The decision became part of the judicial literature of the English speaking world and two Latin words came into common speech, at least among lawyers.

Francis M. Finch became a member of the State Court of Appeals and later dean of the Cornell Law School. Perhaps he is best remembered as a poet. It was he who wrote "The Blue and the Gray," the verse once recited at school exercises every Memorial Day.

In Cornell's regional history collection in Judge Finch's small penciled handwriting is the original draft of "The Blue and the Gray." Also among the Finch papers is a letter written him from a Pennsylvania village. With many a hook and a flourish, the judge's most famous client wrote: "I have been confined in Erie for want of a secure jail in Warren County. Edward H. Rulloff."

The "corpus delicti" decision of 1859 meant that Rulloff must go free unless new evidence was forthcoming. Fifteen years had gone by and there was no new evidence.

The prospect aroused Tompkins County so that

throughout the countryside and in Ithaca was broadcast a poster which read:

"SHALL THE MURDERER GO UNPUNISHED?

"Edward Rulloff will soon gain his freedom unless prompt and effective measures are taken by the people to prevent it.

"Shall this monster be turned loose to glut his tiger appetite for revenge and blood? . . . In the name of humanity, in the name of the relatives of his murdered wife whose heartstrings have been lacerated by this fiend in human shape, in the name of the murdered wife and child, whose pale ghosts call to you from the silent tomb to do your duty, shall the murderer go unpunished?

"We call on those who wish justice done to meet at the Clinton House in Ithaca on Saturday, March 12, 1859, at noon. It will depend upon the action you take that day whether Edward H. Rulloff walks forth a free man or whether he dies the death he so richly deserves."

A battering ram, the size of a telephone pole and requiring 20 men to handle it, was constructed and hidden in Six Mile Creek. Should Sheriff Smith Robertson refuse to deliver his prisoner, the frenzied crowd planned to batter down the door of the jail. Work was also begun on a gallows.

If Rulloff heard the angry voices in the street outside his cell where he was shackled to the floor by chains so heavy they calloused his ankle or heard the hammering on the gallows being built, he gave no sign. Over and again he

78

recited in his rich voice Byron's "Prisoner of Chillon"—in three languages.

Sheriff Robertson determined to prevent the lynching party. On the morning of March 11, a carriage drove up to the jail. The sheriff got in it and drove off alone. The citizens who had been watching the jail left their posts to go to breakfast. The sheriff drove speedily back to the jail and loaded Rulloff into the carriage. Away they went to the steamboat dock.

Just as a Cayuga Lake steamboat was about to take off, sheriff and prisoner leaped aboard. Soon the sheriff had his man safely behind the walls of Auburn Prison.

Five thousand men milled about the Clinton House in frustrated rage. Some wild speeches were made. Threats were heard against the sheriff and Lawyer Finch. But the excitement soon died down. In a few days the man his neighbors had branded "a fiend in human shape" walked forth, a free man.

Rulloff's subsequent career was a strange mixture of scholarly research and crime. He spent considerable time in the New York City Public Library gathering material for a manuscript on "The Origin and Formation of Languages." He also spent considerable time in various jails, usually for burglary.

In a New Hampshire village he masqueraded as a retired Episcopal clergyman, an Oxford graduate. A store in the town was burglarized and stolen goods were found in Rulloff's possession. Sentenced to 10 years in prison, he escaped in three months.

In 1867, as the erudite "Professor Edouardo Leurio," he addressed a convention of the American Philological Association at Vassar College. He read from his manuscript on the formation of languages and the scholarly audience was impressed. But when he tried to collect funds for the publication of his work, he was politely turned down. After that "the professor" turned to crime as more profitable.

Rulloff returned to his old stamping grounds in Central New York in 1869 when he appeared in a Cortland courtroom as attorney for a burglar named Dexter. He had acquired a wealth of knowledge of the law through his bouts with it.

In August, 1870, Rulloff, that same Dexter and Albert Jarvis, who 13 years earlier had let the master criminal out of the jail in Ithaca, went to Binghamton to rob a store.

Their plans miscarried. The two clerks they found sleeping in the store gave battle. Rulloff's gun did away with one of them. The other, although wounded, ran out and spread the alarm. In the early morning a fire bell aroused the Southern Tier city and a manhunt began.

At midnight two of the manhunters spotted a middle-aged, scholarly appearing man walking the railroad tracks. He was carrying a satchel and an umbrella. Ordered to halt, Rulloff managed to put a passing coal train between himself and his pursuers. He was soon captured and taken back to Binghamton.

The bodies of his two accomplices were found floating in the Susquehanna River. Rulloff vowed he had never seen either of them before. Bruises on the bodies indicated that Rulloff had put them out of the way to make his own escape easier.

While he was being questioned, the judge who had presided at his Tioga County trial came into the room and recognized the prisoner. To his "Aren't you Rulloff?" he got an affirmative reply. But Rulloff coolly told his questioners that it was merely a coincidence that he happened to be in a town where a burglary and murder had been committed. He talked so convincingly that he was released.

A pair of shoes he had left behind in the store as he fled proved his undoing. The left shoe showed an indentation over the big toe. Someone recalled that Rulloff had frozen a foot during one of his jail breaks and that the great toe of his left foot had been amputated.

Again the hunt was on. Again he was caught as he walked the railroad tracks. This time he was not freed. The left shoe of the pair found at the murder scene fitted his deformed foot exactly.

Rulloff was tried and convicted of murder. He appealed to prominent people over all the country to save the life of "a scholar who has discovered a universal language." The gullible New York editor, Horace Greeley, visited him in his cell and was impressed. But Gov. John T. Hoffman was deaf to all appeals for commutation of sentence.

A lunacy commission examined Rulloff and found him sane. One doctor later described him as having unbounded egotism and little genuine learning. Once he almost persuaded a sheriff not to handcuff him while he was shifted from one jail to another. After refusing the plea, the sheriff asked: "If you could escape by killing me, would you do it?" Calmly Rulloff replied: "I would kill you like a dog."

He was an infidel and to the last spurned all religious counsel. It was said he spent his last night on earth boasting of his knowledge and uttering blasphemies.

Edward Rulloff was hanged in Binghamton before a large crowd on May 18, 1871. His last act, although involuntary, was spectacular. When he went to the gallows, his arms were pinioned at the elbows with a rope across his back and his hands were thrust in his trousers pockets. As the trap was sprung, his right hand was yanked out of his pocket. His neck was broken but that hand was raised as if in farewell.

After the Governor had turned down his appeal for commutation, Rulloff said: "I shall be remembered long after Hoffman is gone. He will be remembered only as a scheming politician, I as the author of one of the grandest theories on the formation of language."

He was partly right. The Tammany Governor is forgotten. Edward H. Rulloff is remembered, not as the author of any grand theory of philology, but as "The Fiend of the Finger Lakes."

Chapter 10

First Woman Minister

A historical marker stands in front of the big house of warmly tinted fieldstone that "Squire" Joseph Brown built in 1831 on Pinnacle Road in the Monroe County town of Henrietta.

Farmer Brown, who was a justice of the peace, hence known as "Squire" to the neighborhood, needed a big house because he and his wife, Abby, had 10 children.

The seventh of those children became one of America's most famous woman trail blazers. The marker tells the passerby that the sturdy old stone house was the early home of Antoinette Brown Blackwell, the first ordained woman minister in the United States.

Before her girlhood dream came true, she had to conquer a wall of prejudice, even the opposition of her own family. In mid-19th Century, the mere idea of a woman in the pulpit was almost unthinkable.

Antoinette, who became Nettie to her friends, was born in 1825 in a double log house near the present fieldstone landmark with its cellar walls built into the side of a hill.

Unpublished memoirs in the possession of Henrietta Town Historian Eleanor Kalsbeck, tell of a happy girlhood, roaming the woods and fields, climbing trees, learning the names of the animals, as well as those of passing Indians. Whenever the Brown children "played church," Nettie always wanted the part of the minister, it was recalled in later years.

Nettie attended a little district school before she entered the historic Monroe Academy in Henrietta. At the age of nine she became a member of her family's Congregational Church.

When she was 15, she left the Academy to teach district schools, "boarding around" with farm families, as was the custom in those days. She saved her money for future college expenses while her ambition to preach the Gospel became more and more obsessive. But Nettie kept her dream locked in her heart, not daring to tell others about it.

She was an attractive, healthy girl, popular in the neighborhood, and she did not lack male admirers. She rejected one youth's proposal because marriage did not fit in with her plans.

In 1846, with some financial help from her father, Nettie enrolled in the ladies' literary course at Oberlin in Ohio, the first co-educational college and the first to admit Negroes.

In her senior year Antionette Brown revealed to her family and to the college faculty her intention to study theology. Her father, shocked at her audacity, withdrew his support. Her brother, William, an ordained minister, strongly opposed her plan.

The Oberlin faculty, because of the college's liberal charter, could not prohibit her from attending theological classes. But it would not allow her to register. The girl from Henrietta worked as a housekeeper and taught art classes to defray expenses.

On completion of the two-year theological course, her application for a license to preach was rejected as "reckless and blasphemous." She was told to "preach or be silent on her own responsibility." And this reputedly liberal college denied her participation in the graduation exercises.

At this crisis in her life, Lucy Stone, who had been her most intimate friend at Oberlin, came to the rescue. Miss Stone, who was destined for fame as a reformer, invited Nettie to speak at a suffrage convention in Worcester, Mass.

Her platform debut was a success. She was asked to speak at abolition, temperance and equal rights meetings. More important to her were the occasional chances she had to preach.

In the winter of 1852–53 she joined Susan B. Anthony and Amelia Bloomer as paid lecturers for the New York State Temperance Society. Their tour included Rochester, where they spoke in old Corinthian Hall.

On July 4, 1853 Nettie Brown spoke at the holiday celebration at South Butler, a Wayne County village which was to mark an important milestone in her career.

The next Sunday she preached in New York City. In her

audience was the noted editor, Horace Greeley, who was so impressed that he offered her $1,000 a year to preach in Metropolitan Hall.

Antoinette turned down the tempting offer because she wanted to begin her ministry in a small place where she would know and live among her people, rather than in a big city with its impersonal audiences.

Soon the call she desired came. It was from the little Congregational flock at South Butler and the salary was $300 a year. Nettie accepted the offer gladly.

Her dream came true on Sept. 15, 1853 when she was ordained to the ministry in the village church, blazing a new trail for her sex. Gerrit Smith, a leader in all reform movements, attended the service. Greeley could not come but he sent two reporters to cover the historic event. At the age of 26 the girl from Henrietta became the first ordained woman minister in America.

But she found her rural pastorate no bed of roses. Not all of her congregation accepted her concept of a compassionate Deity. They clung to the old doctrine of hell and brimstone as punishment for sinners. Some could not reconcile themselves to the idea of a woman pastor.

Nettie stayed in South Butler only one year. While she was there, she had met young Samuel Blackwell, whose sister, Elizabeth, was the first woman physician in the land, receiving her degree from the old Geneva Medical College in 1849.

On Jan. 24, 1856 in the stone house in Henrietta Squire

Brown united his daughter and Sam Blackwell in marriage.

Soon after the marriage, Sam sold out his hardware business in Cincinnati and the couple moved to the New York–New Jersey area. They raised four daughters, one child dying in infancy. Nettie found time to lecture on social reforms and to write several books and essays.

She often saw her college friend, Lucy Stone, who had married Henry Blackwell, Sam's brother, but insisted on retaining her maiden name, exhorting other women to follow her example. She created a vogue among feminists who were known as "Lucy Stoners."

At the age of 75 Antoinette Blackwell began a 15-year pastorate in an Elizabeth, N.J., Unitarian church. She journeyed to the Holy Land when she was 78 and two years later visited Alaska.

Oberlin College made amends for its shabby treatment of its onetime student, granting Nettie a master of arts degree in 1878 and a doctor of divinity degree in 1908 when she was 83.

After fighting for suffrage since her girlhood, she cast her first ballot in a presidential election in 1920, when she was 95.

The next year death claimed this remarkable woman. Memorial and cremation services were held in Elizabeth.

In the twilight of her years, her memories must often have strayed back to her girlhood in Henrietta and its pastoral serenity. The old stone house where she lived in

her youth and the Monroe Academy, no longer a temple of
learning, still stand. Otherwise Antoinette Brown Blackwell would find few familiar landmarks of her home town
in the fast-growing industrial-residential suburb of today.

Chapter 11

"On to Richmond!"

"The Congressmen went out to Bull Run,
The Congressmen who like free shows and spectacles."
From "John Brown's Body" by Stephen Vincent Benet

*   *   *

A warm sun shone down on Washington on Sunday, July 21, 1861. As yet there had been no decisive battle in the Civil War. For months the Northern press had been screaming: "On to Richmond!"

Now at long last the Blue and the Gray were to join battle, along a winding, sluggish Virginia stream called Bull Run. It was 20 miles from Washington.

A holiday atmosphere prevailed in the Union capital. Members of Congress and other high-placed civilians left for Virginia early in the morning to "see the Rebels run."

As Benet wrote in his epic poem of the Civil War:

"They brought their wives and carriages along,
They brought their speeches and their picnic lunch,
Some brought a little whiskey, too
(A little whiskey is a comforting thing)

89

For Congressmen in the sun, in the heat of the sun,
For bearded Congressmen with orator's mouths,
The fine, clean-shaven Congressmen
Come out to see the gladiator's show. . . ."

Among the Congressmen who rode out to Bull Run that July Sunday as light heartedly as if he were bound for a picnic at Charlotte was the Hon. Alfred Ely of Rochester, representing the 38th New York District.

He belonged to the "fine, clean-shaven" type of Congressmen. He took no women folk along; probably he took no whiskey either. He was a dignified family man, a substantial citizen. He lived in the Third Ward, the domain of the "Ruffled Shirts," and he was a communicant of St. Luke's. Alfred Ely was a proper Rochesterian.

He had come from his native Connecticut to the young mill town–canal port of Rochester in 1836, had built up a flourishing law business and in 1858 had been elected to Congress as a Union Republican. Now in 1861 at the age of 46 he was serving his second term.

Rochester's own 13th Regiment was among the raw troops of McDowell's command which faced the equally untried forces of Beauregard that July day in '61. Congressman Ely states the motive for his visit to Bull Run in different fashion than poet Benet. Because the battle pushed him into the limelight, the Rochester politician later wrote "The Journal of Alfred Ely, a Prisoner of War in Richmond," which began:

"On Saturday, July 20, 1861, participating with many

others in the anxiety of the day and curious to witness what should occur, I applied to Gen. Winfield Scott in Washington for a passport to visit our troops, then encamped at Fairfax Court House and Centreville, near what is known as Bull Run where it was expected a battle would take place on the following day."

So Congressman Ely put on a fresh white linen coat and hired a carriage for $25, a lot of money in 1861. Along with him to see the Rebel rout went U.S. Senator Foster of Connecticut, a sutler from the 13th Regiment, a Lieutenant Ash and "an Italian gentleman" named Bing.

"We left Washington at 5 A.M. in a double carriage drawn by fine horses, with our provisions for the day laid in and our company apparently in high spirits," the Congressman related in his journal.

> *"The huge innocent army, ready to fight*
> *But only half taught the tricks of fighting,*
> *Ready to die like picture-post card boys*
> *While fighting had banners and a sword,*
> *And just as ready to run in blind mob panic,*
> *Salutes with a vast and thunderous cry,*
> *Ave, Caesar: ave O Congressmen,*
> *Ave, Iliad gods who forced the fight,*
> *You bring your carriage and your picnic lunch*
> *To cheer us in our need."*

At Centreville the Ely party ran into several members of Congress. The dusty road to Bull Run was choked with civilian carriages. Near its destination the Ely equipage was sideswiped by an Army wagon and a wheel was disabled. Senator Foster left the carriage. It was five months before Ely saw him again. The others of the party wandered off while the Congressman went with the driver to a blacksmith shop for repairs to the carriage.

After the wheel was fixed, Ely encountered two fellow Rochesterians, also sightseeing in the war zone. They were D. D. S. Brown, editor of an agricultural journal, and Calvin Huson, Jr., a former district attorney whom Ely had beaten in a Congress race. The two were good friends for all of that.

Then Alfred Ely, with a fine disregard for his personal safety, strolled down the road toward the battlefield. He was closer than he thought. A rifle ball struck uncomfortably near him and he took shelter behind the trunk of a large tree. He stood there a long time. "A cannon ball came crashing through the branches, scattering leaves and adding to my alarm," he wrote in a later year.

"And when the fight is done, your carriages
Will bear you safely through the streaming rout
Of broken troops, throwing their guns away."

But Congressman Ely of Rochester, in his immaculate white linen coat, his locks worn long in the statesman fashion, was not borne safely away in his double carriage. He never saw "the streaming rout of broken troops, throwing their guns away" in the Union debacle that was Bull Run.

For as he watched from his tree shelter, he saw a company of troops advance from a dense wood. They wore uniforms of gray. An officer on horseback was at their head. They halted about 10 rods from Ely and his tree.

They saw the man in the white coat standing there. Two officers came up, and after learning that the civilian under the tree was a "Yankee Congressman," they seized him and took away the pistol he had borrowed from the Union sutler. Ely was taken before a Confederate colonel who threatened to "blow out his brains." More chivalrous Rebel officers interposed.

Twilight found the road back to Washington clogged with panic-stricken troops in blue. Their flight was impeded somewhat by the carriages of the Congressmen. Maybe the one Ely had hired was in the scramble. Definitely Congressman Ely was not.

He was being marched, the only civilian among 600 Union officers and men, all prisoners of war, to Manassas, seven miles over "the dustiest road it was ever my fortune to travel." He was thirsty and he drank with the other prisoners from a dirty pool along the road.

The prisoners were taken to "a miserable old barn," which was already crowded. There "without any blanket or covering other than a light linen coat upon my back, I passed the night. And such a night," wrote the Congressman who lived in a fine big house in Rochester's "Ruffled Shirt" ward and in Willard's Hotel in Washington.

93

His white linen coat was a sorry mess.

Northern editors and politicos had long been shrilling: "On to Richmond." Congressman Ely was the first Northern politician to reach the Confederate capital in 1861.

With the 600 other prisoners, he was taken by train to Richmond. They were marched under guard through the quiet moonlit streets of the Virginia city to an old brick former tobacco factory, later to be known as Libby Prison and to live in infamy.

Ely's journal reveals the gentleman from New York's 38th District as a man of restraint, dignity, compassion and considerable courage. He made no complaint of ill treatment of himself although he related incidents of cruelty toward enlisted men and of generally wretched conditions in the Rebel prison.

Right away Ely prepared a petition to President Lincoln, asking immediate action toward effecting the release of himself and his fellow prisoners "through exchange or other means." His petition seems to have been ignored, but the Congressman never showed any resentment toward Lincoln. The paper may have never reached the President's desk.

"The Yankee Congressman" who had been bagged at Bull Run attracted as much attention as a caged lion or a circus freak. Southerners whom he had known in Congress, generals and hundreds of merely curious people, ladies among them, flocked to the prison to see Alfred Ely. One of them brought him a new dark frock coat to replace "the thin white linen coat that I had on which had become horribly soiled."

His sartorial squalor seems to have bothered the Congressman more than the coarse food, the tin cup, wooden plate, lack of any pillow "except an oval block of wood which grew tolerably soft as our acquaintance increased" or "sleeping on the naked floor."

The Southern press jeered at his plight and one newspaper demanded that "the Hon. Mr. Ely be ironed and sent to Fort Sumter and there kept in a dungeon until the captain of the *Savannah* is released." The crew of the *Savannah,* a Southern privateer, had been seized and was being held in prison in New York.

Ely's journal tells of the Richmond Prison Association formed by the prisoners "for their improvement and amusement." He was its president. He also records his joy over the occasional letters that reached him from home and the "photograph likeness of daughter Carrie;" his grief over "the sleepless nights which my imprudence must have occasioned my wife." At that point he admits that tears stained the page.

On the second day of the Congressman's imprisonment, he was joined by his personal friend and political foe, Calvin Huson. While looking for Ely, Huson had fallen into Confederate hands.

Huson was stricken with typhoid fever and after a lingering illness died in the Richmond prison. Ely had worked hard for Huson's release and lamented that his friend could not have received better care. In August another Monroe County man, John B. Nichols of Spencerport, died in the prison hospital. He had been wounded at Bull Run and his leg had been amputated. Congressman Ely took care of the burial of his constituent.

On Sept. 12 Ely recorded that there was no more coffee or sugar on the prison menu because of shortages. He rejoiced to know that the Union blockade was succeeding.

Through an exchange of prisoners, the Rochester Congressman was freed on Christmas Day of 1861. His train arrived in Washington on the night of Dec. 27 and crowds cheered him on his way from the station to Willard's Hotel.

In the Confederate capital he had been an object of derisive curiosity. In the capital of the Union he was something of a hero. He addressed a crowd from the balcony of his hotel that night and the band played "Home, Sweet Home."

After his release from his five months imprisonment, Ely devoted much time and effort to the cause of the Union war prisoners and made several speeches telling of the misery he had seen in Libby Prison.

But back in Rochester, his "home, sweet home," the Republicans denied him a renomination for Congress in 1862. His political career was closed but he still had his lucrative law practice. He died in 1892 in the big brick mansion at Plymouth Avenue and Troup Street.

Alfred Ely, the "Yankee Congressman" who, captured by the Rebels as he crouched behind a tree at the Battle of Bull Run, deserves a footnote in history. Involuntary as his action was, he was the first Northern politician to respond to the popular cry, "On to Richmond," in the first Summer of the four-year Civil War.

For all his long stay in Libby Prison, fate was kinder to him than to the Massachusetts Senator who had to ride a mule back to Washington amid the rabble after the Union debacle at Bull Run.

Chapter 12

A Spy in Their Midst

It was with heavy hearts that the parishioners of St. Mary's in Canandaigua gathered for Mass in the old church on Saltonstall Street on the Easter Sunday of 1865.

It should have been the first joyous Easter in four sad war-torn years. Only the week before, the bells had rung out the news of Lee's surrender, of Union victory and the doom of the Confederacy. But now the bells tolled the dirge and in place of the gay bunting, hung in the hour of triumph, black streamers floated down from buildings in the Finger Lakes city.

For Abraham Lincoln lay dead in the East Room of the White House, the victim of an assassin. His Secretary of State, William Henry Seward of Auburn, had been stabbed on his sick bed. Vice President Andrew Johnson and Gen. U. S. Grant, also marked for death, had escaped.

Grief for the murdered Lincoln and anger against the beaten South mounted to hysteria pitch throughout the North as the plot to kill the heads of state was unfolded.

In Maryland and in Virginia a grim hunt was on for the

handsome actor, John Wilkes Booth, who had escaped
from Ford's Theater in Washington after shooting the
President on the night of Good Friday, April 14, 1865.

Others named as conspirators had been rounded up. But
the man accused as second to Booth in the plot was still at
large. His name was John Harrison Surratt, Jr., and although he was only 21 years old, he had been a Confederate courier and spy for four years.

A wild rumor was afloat that it was Surratt who had
stabbed Secretary Seward and felled four members of his
household. An uncouth giant, Lewis Payne, later was
hanged for that crime.

Among those who knelt in old St. Mary's Church in
Canandaigua that Easter morning of 1865 was a tall, fair-
haired, well groomed young man, a stranger to the community. Little did his fellow worshipers dream that the
stranger in their midst was the much-wanted John Surratt.

The night before he had come to town from Elmira and
had registered at the Webster House under the name of
John Harrison. He was beginning a two-year flight which
was to take him to faraway lands and into strange adventures before he was finally captured and brought to trial.

The presence of Surratt in Upstate New York before
and after the assassination of Lincoln has been revealed by
the long and patient research of a Rochester housewife.
Mrs. Margaret Kahler Bearden, a niece of Hugh McNair
Kahler, the magazine writer, for 12 years dug into old
records and shared notes with other Civil War historians.

In her study of the conspiracy, she had concentrated on

the parts played in the drama by John Surratt and his widowed mother who died on the gallows, the first American woman ever executed by the government. Today many believe her to have been the innocent victim of mass hysteria, political malice and of circumstances.

Mrs. Bearden found accounts of Surratt's visit to New York State in the voluminous record of his trial in 1867 which ended in a jury disagreement and his release. No doubt he owed his freedom to his alibi—that he was in Elmira the night Lincoln was shot.

Maryland-born John Surratt was only 17 when he began serving the Confederacy as a dispatch carrier between Washington and rebel boats on the Potomac. His mother, an ardent Secessionist, had abandoned a village tavern in Maryland 13 miles from Washington to open a boarding house in the capital city.

In the Fall of 1864 young Surratt met the fascinating actor, John Wilkes Booth, and came under his spell. By his own admission, he became involved with Booth and others in a fantastic plot to kidnap Lincoln as the President rode in his carriage to the Soldiers' Home on the outskirts of Washington. Surratt, Booth and four others rode out to lay in wait for the President.

They planned to demand the release of all Confederate prisoners in exchange for the captured Lincoln. The scheme was a flop. Lincoln did not ride that day and the conspirators returned to the Surratt boarding house, chagrined and empty handed.

Surratt maintained to his dying day that he never saw

Booth after March 18, 1865 and that he knew nothing about any plan to kill the President.

On April 3, 1865, two days before the fall of Richmond, he left the Rebel capital with dispatches from Secretary of War Judah P. Benjamin to Gen. E. G. Lee at Canadian headquarters in Montreal. There Lee gave him a new assignment.

Young Surratt was to proceed to Elmira, N.Y., gain entry to the big Federal war prison there, make sketches of the place and gather all other information needed for a wholesale jail-break. Seemingly Canadian headquarters did not realize that the Confederacy was on its last legs.

On arrival in Elmira on April 12, Surratt registered at the Brainard House, later the Rathbun, as "John Harrison" and mingled freely with the many officers in blue who were his fellow guests. By bribing one of them, he got into the sprawling prison camp which housed 20,000 Confederates, made his sketches and gathered his data.

On April 13, his 21st birthday, he bought a suit of clothes in an Elmira store. Alterations had to be made and he was told to come back for the garments later. The Elmira merchant, his bookkeeper and his cutter, along with another clothier, were important defense witnesses two years later in Surratt's trial.

As he related in after years, he retired Good Friday night at 10 in the Brainard House (Lincoln was shot at 10:22), "little thinking that on that night a blow would be struck which would forever blast my hopes and make me a wanderer in a foreign land."

The next morning he learned from the excited talk at the breakfast table that Lincoln had been slain. No assailant was named. Surratt maintained that never for a moment did he associate Booth with the deed.

However, the disturbing news caused him to revise his plans. He would return at once to Richmond. A Spring freshest had washed out railroad tracks in the Southern Tier and he found he would have to travel via New York.

Three months earlier, he had stayed with Booth in New York at the home of the actor's relatives and he planned to stop over there again in case Booth was in the city.

At the telegraph office in the lobby of the Brainard, Surratt wrote out this dispatch: "J.W.B. If you are in New York, telegraph me. John Harrison." The operator had hardly finished pounding out the message when Surratt heard some appalling news from four chattering women who had entered the hotel lobby. They were talking about "that actor Booth who killed the President."

Surratt was stunned. He sensed his own grave danger and vainly tried to retrieve his message to Booth. He resolved on flight to Canada and, packing his carpetbag, left Elmira by train for Canandaigua. He planned to go on to Rochester and there board a Lake Ontario boat for Cobourg, Ontario.

After registering at the Webster House in Canandaigua, he learned to his dismay that the Rochester-Cobourg boat did not run Sundays. It must have been a desperately worried young man who knelt in the church (now long gone from the scene) that Easter Sunday.

The register of the Webster House, now in the archives of the War Department, figured in Surratt's defense. The name, "John Harrison," is there, smack in the center of the page. But the presiding judge would not admit it as evidence, holding that the name could have been written in later.

The Brainard House register mysteriously disappeared. Federal agents had been busy. It would have been valuable defense evidence.

On Monday, April 17, Surratt left Canandaigua, to return by rail to Elmira, thence to make the long journey to Montreal by way of St. Albans, the Vermont border town once raided by men in gray.

The next two years were packed with adventure for the fugitive. For five months he found refuge in Canada. In the meantime John Wilkes Booth had been shot to death as he emerged from a blazing barn in Virginia. Surratt's mother and three men had gone to the gallows as conspirators in Lincoln's murder. They had been hastily tried by a military commission in an atmosphere of hate and vengeance.

John Surratt crossed the ocean, became a soldier in the Papal Zouves under an assumed name, made his escape from Rome by leaping a deep ravine when his identity was discovered and then fled to Egypt, where he was apprehended and returned to the United States.

He went on trial in Washington on June 10, 1867 before a jury, half Rebel, half Yankee. The prosecution tried to place him in Washington on April 14 and 15,

1865. Defense counsel, after declaring "we will show he was not within 400 miles of Washington on those days," put his alibi witnesses, including the four Elmirans, and Surratt's superior officer, Gen. E. G. Lee, on the stand.

After two days of debate, the jury disagreed in August, with eight members voting for acquittal. Surratt was kept in prison until June, 1868. Three months later the charge was nolle prossed and he was set free.

Except for a brief and unsuccessful lecture tour in which he told his strange story, Surratt lived quietly in Maryland the rest of his days. For nearly 50 years he was auditor for a steamship line. John Harrison Surratt was 72 when he was claimed by death in 1916.

There is no record that he ever revisited "the enemy country" of Upstate New York which he had entered as a spy in 1865.

Yet often his memories must have turned to the prison camp at Elmira, the city where first he heard of Lincoln's death; to an Easter Sunday when he attended Mass in a stately old town named Canandaigua, an Easter Sunday when the boats did not run from Rochester to Cobourg.

Chapter 13

Churchill's Upstate Heritage

"Winston Churchill was so British. He was the personification of John Bull."

Such a statement tempts one to explode with a so American phrase: "Oh, yeah?" For, let it not be forgotten, the British statesman, the towering figure of his times, was half American.

In his veins was the blood of many an English duke. So also was the blood of many an Upstate New York pioneer. None of the latter was as famous as John Churchill, the warrior first Duke of Marlborough. But Winston Churchill had no need to be ashamed of any of his American forebears. His maternal grandfather, Leonard Jerome, cut quite a figure in his day and he was as colorful as any duke.

The late Prime Minister's full name was Winston Leonard Spencer Churchill. The Leonard was for the grandfather who rose from Upstate farm boy to become one of New York's most dazzling millionaires.

Perhaps Sir Winston inherited some of his flair for

politics from his great-grandfather, Ambrose Hall, who in the 1820s was Palmyra's highway commissioner and a member of the State Assembly.

Rene Kraus, one of the Churchill biographers, ascribes to the American strain in "Winnie's" blood characteristics of "shrewdness, keenness, talent for self advertisement and sense of humor."

One wonders if Churchill did not also inherit his audacity, his gusto and his gift for the pungent phrase from ancestors who were Upstate pioneers.

One of them was David Wilcox, native of Massachusetts, who in 1791 came with his wife and two children to the raw new settlement of Palmyra, poling his boat through the narrow creek called by the Indians, Ganargua, and by the pioneers, plain Mud Creek. He was then 28 and a blacksmith, as well as a farmer. He bought 100 acres of land for $125. He died in Macedon in 1828. That is all that is known about David Wilcox.

He figures in the Churchill story because he had a comely daughter named Clarissa. In 1818, when she was 21 years old, a thirsty hunter came to her door and she gave him a drink of water.

The hunter's name was Ambrose Hall of Williamstown, Mass. He was Clarissa's senior by 21 years. The chance meeting blossomed into romance and on Christmas Eve of the next year they were married by the Presbyterian minister in Palmyra.

They lived, first on a farm at Baptist and Quaker Roads, north of Palmyra, and later on the site of the present village park. Ambrose Hall became a man of consequence, owner of several farms and of a valuable strip of land along the main street of Palmyra, which boomed with the completion of the Erie Canal in 1825. Hall was 51 when he died in 1827, three months after his wife.

They rest in the cemetery on the hill above the canal town. There is a substantial monument on the well kept lot, which is surrounded by an iron fence. There are headstones for Ambrose, his wife and two of their five daughters who died young. Another daughter, Caroline, is buried there, beside her husband, the Rev. Fay Purdy.

Two other daughters are buried elsewhere. They married two dashing young brothers from over Marion way who won fame and fortune in later years far from the strange-shaped hills of Wayne. Katherine married Lawrence Jerome. The other, Clarissa, married Leonard Jerome. Leonard and Clarissa had a daughter, Jennie, who became the bride of Lord Randolph Churchill and bore him a son named Winston.

The Jeromes were of English stock. The first one in America, Timothy, came to New England from the Isle of Wight around 1709.

Early in the next century, a descendant, Isaac Jerome, was living on a farm in Pompey, Onondaga County. He had married Aurora Murray of Chatham in 1807. She was of Scottish descent and like a celebrated great-grandson, was described as lively and ambitious. Her husband served in the county militia and rose to a captaincy.

To them, between 1808 and 1830, eleven children, nine

sons and two daughters, were born. The fifth son, Leonard W., arrived on Nov. 3, 1817. Pompey, the old town on the Cherry Valley Turnpike near Syracuse, also is the birthplace of Horatio Seymour, twice governor of New York and Democratic candidate for the Presidency in 1868.

According to tradition, the house in which Leonard Jerome was born was long ago moved back from the road and became a part of the long barn on the farm.

From that farm young Leonard Jerome trudged to the village school. He grew into a tall, handsome youth who had a way with him. He had a soaring ambition and was determined to get a good education.

At the age of 19 he entered Princeton where he had to work his way. After two years he transferred to Union College from which he was graduated in 1839. Reminiscences of classmates pictured him as companionable, attractive and hard working.

Around 1837 the Isaac Jeromes and their numerous offspring moved to a farm on the Eddy Ridge–Hall Corners Road northwest of Marion. There Isaac apparently was a tenant farmer, as no deeds are on record to show he was a land owner.

Probably he moved to Wayne County because his brother, Hiram K. Jerome, lived and practiced law in Palmyra. Hiram was appointed county judge in 1840. After graduation from Union College, Leonard Jerome read law in his uncle's office.

Leonard and his younger brother, Lawrence, drove high stepping horses and fancy rigs. They were popular among the Palmyra belles, including Katherine and Clarissa Hall. The Hall sisters had good looks and had inherited considerable property.

Larry Jerome married Katherine Hall in August, 1844. Later that year they and brother Leonard moved to Rochester, where Uncle Hiram took the brothers into his law office.

The brothers displayed little liking or aptitude for the law and in 1845 they bought into the Rochester *Daily American*, a Whig newspaper. Their parents came on from Marion and father Isaac and one of his sons worked on the paper. Leonard boarded with the Larry Jeromes in a brick house on South Fitzhugh Street, in the then swank Third Ward.

Leonard Jerome married Clarissa Hall at Palmyra in April, 1849, and the two young couples lived in the Fitzhugh Street house.

The two families were active in Third Ward social events and in Whig politics. Larry was the gayer of the brothers and delighted in practical jokes. Leonard was more dignified and full of grandiose plans.

In 1850 the Jeromes sold their interest in the *American*. Leonard was rewarded for his loyalty to the new President, Millard Fillmore, by appointment as United States consul to Ravenna, Italy. He never filled the post but instead moved to Brooklyn where he became associated with the booming telegraph industry. In 1852 he assumed the consulate post at Trieste, Italy. There he remained only 16 months. The new President, Franklin Pierce, was not interested in faithful Whigs.

Lawrence Jerome stayed in Rochester until 1855, when he moved to New York. A son, William Travers Jerome, got into the headlines around the turn of the century as a crusading district attorney.

By 1858 all the Jeromes had left Rochester. Last to go was Hiram, who returned to Palmyra where until recent years his little, old fashioned, one-story law office stood on Market Street.

After Winston Churchill became a world figure, a spirited rivalry developed between Rochester and Brooklyn as to which city was the birthplace of his mother. Lady Randolph Churchill, who should know, stated flatly in her autobiography that "I was born in Brooklyn."

Still some Rochesterians persisted in their claim until City Historian Blake McKelvey, whose passion for accuracy transcends "civic pride," presented conclusive evidence that Jennie Jerome had been born in Brooklyn in 1854.

Before the Fitzhugh Street house was torn down to make way for Rochester's Civic Center, a bronze tablet had been placed on it, stating that "the grandfather of Winston Churchill resided here."

When in 1941 the University of Rochester awarded Churchill an honorary degree through the medium of radio, the tactful politician said in his response: "As you tell me, my mother was born in Rochester." Later he confirmed Brooklyn's claim in a congratulatory message.

110

While on his two visits to Rochester to fill speaking engagements, first in 1901 when he was a Boer War hero and again in the 1930s, when he was out of office and a voice crying in the wilderness to smug Britain of Nazi danger, Churchill never bothered to visit any of the places where his grandparents had lived.

However, the British statesman seemed to have a real feeling for Leonard and Clarissa Jerome, whose portraits graced his bedroom, and Churchill wrote in an admiring vein of his American grandfather.

That grandfather was no ordinary American. He was a spectacular figure in the New York of his day. He made a fortune in the stock market during the Civil War, lost it and made another. When he was owner of the New York *Times,* he armed his staff during the wartime draft riots to defend his office against the mobs.

Leonard Jerome, tall, dark, impeccably groomed, handsomely mustached, did everything on a grand scale. He was one of the founders of the American Jockey Club and its race track was named Jerome Park. With August Belmont, he introduced four-in-hand driving in New York and dazzled the metropolis with the elegance of his turnouts and the lavishness of his parties.

His stables were as magnificent as his mansion on Madison Square. He became a patron of the arts, an "angel" for rising singers and actresses, particularly pretty ones. And this sophisticate had been born on a farm on Pompey Hill!

The four Jerome daughters were reared in luxury, educated abroad and traveled widely.

It came to pass that on a moonlight night in 1873 that a grand ball was held aboard a British man of war in the harbor of Cowes. Among the guests was a lissome American girl of 19, whose slim Grecian face was crowned with dark curls. Another guest was the 24-year-old son of the seventh Duke of Marlborough, five years out of Oxford.

Lord Randolph Churchill danced the first quadrille with the dark-haired American girl to whom he had just been introduced. Then came a waltz. The young peer disliked waltzes. "Let's walk this out," he suggested. The couple walked three times around the deck, bathed in moonlight. Later Lord Randolph said to a friend: "See those two girls standing there? That dark one I will make my wife."

He kept his word, despite some objections by his parents, whose opposition to the match melted when they learned the size of the Jerome fortune. Lord Randolph Churchill and Jennie Jerome were married on April 15, 1874.

It had been a love match with them. So had it been with Jennie's grandparents: Ambrose Hall, the thirsty hunter, and Clarissa Wilcox, the blacksmith's daughter, who had given a stranger a drink of water at Palmyra in the backwoods so many years before.

Chapter 14

Links with the White House

The farming–salt mining Town of York in the Genesee Valley seems far removed from the glamor that surrounds the White House.

While its name has a ducal connotation, it only honors Joseph C. York, the North Country Assemblyman who sponsored the legislation which created the township in 1819.

Yet in that township there are tangible links with at least three First Families of the land.

One is the name the widow of a President scratched on a window pane of a mansion which has faced the winding Genesee for more than a century.

Another is a once gracious mansion hidden in a wood. There once a President and his lively daughter came to ride to hounds in the Genesee Valley. There also some First Ladies of the stage were guests. Now, sad to relate this palatial residence houses a liquor store.

Exhibit 3 is a low brick building in York village, which is some 145 years old and may collapse any day now. It was once a schoolhouse and a future President conned his boyhood lessons there—as a plaque in front of the long vacant building proclaims.

One of the few manor houses left in the Valley of the Genesee is Westerly, where Porter Chandler, the New York lawyer, spends his Summer vacations and some weekends. He chose its name because his estate lies on the westerly side of the valley where he was born.

Before his time, it was known as the Charles Wadsworth place and some of the finest Short Horn cattle in the nation cropped the grass on the river bottoms.

Under spreading oaks and tall hickory trees stands the mansion with its spacious, vine-covered porch, pillared porte-cochere, tall end chimneys and green blinds at every window.

It is on one of those windows that the name "Julia G. Tyler" still can be seen. The widow of John Tyler, the 10th President, scratched her name on the pane in the 1870s.

Julia Gardiner, comely daughter of an old New York family, married the middle-aged Tyler, a widower, in 1844 at a quiet ceremony in New York. They had met on the ill-fated cruise of the U.S.S. *Princeton* on the Potomac, when a gun exploded while firing a salute, killing five persons, including two Cabinet members and former Senator David Gardiner, Julia's father. The 50-year-old President was attracted to the bereaved young lady and their courtship was formal and brief.

Skillfully the 22-year-old bride presided over the social life of the White House for Tyler's remaining seven months as Chief Executive. John Tyler, the Virginia planter, died in 1862 while serving in the Confederate Congress.

He fathered 15 children, eight by his first wife and seven by his second. The third child of the second marriage, born in 1849, was named Julia after her mother. In 1849 she married William H. Spencer, Jr., son of the pioneer merchant who had built Westerly.

Young Spencer and his bride moved into the Valley house, and in the Spring of 1871 Julia Gardiner Tyler came there to care for her daughter, who was expecting a child.

It was during her stay that she scratched her name on the window with a diamond ring. She started her name on a second pane but never finished it. Maybe she did it in a moment of abstraction or loneliness, for the Genesee Valley was a quiet place for one used to the glitter of Washington. She left before tragedy struck.

A few hours after Julia Spencer gave birth to a daughter, the mansion caught fire from a defective fireplace. She and her newly-born babe were carried from the burning house. A bucket brigade easily put out the fire but shock and exposure cost the life of a daughter of a President. The fireplace was not used for 50 years after the tragedy.

The motherless baby, christened Julia, was adopted by an aunt who lived for a time at the Spencer home. Never again did the former First Lady visit the manor house in Western New York, fraught with such sad memories.

But her name is still on the window pane.

* * *

Wolcott Road seems to the casual traveler just another side road. Many never see the mansion which sits far back from the highway and is well hidden by trees and shrubbery.

Go up its long and winding drive and your first view of Hillcrest, even today in its decline, is breath taking. You never expected to see such an elaborate estate in a back road setting.

Some famous folk have traveled that tree-lined drive. One was Theodore Roosevelt. The Rough Rider came first before the turn of the century when he was Governor of New York. A few years later, when he was President, he and his daughter, "Princess" Alice, cantered up that path after riding in the Genesee Valley Hunt as guests of a member of the Wadsworth clan.

Other celebrities were guests at Hillcrest in the days when Mrs. Frances Wolcott was mistress of the mansion. She was a cultivated, widely traveled lady, the wife of a wealthy U.S. Senator from Colorado, Edward O. Wolcott. The Senator never crossed the threshold of Hillcrest. By the time the mansion was built in 1898–99, he and his wife had reached the parting of the ways.

It was an imposing country estate which rose on acres thrifty Scotch pioneers had tilled. The first story of the

116

main residence is of stone and the second story of brown shingles. It contains 27 rooms, including 17 bedrooms, five fireplaces and a central room 40 by 70 feet.

Add an eight-room guest house, barns, stables (now garages), a swimming pool, a bath house, a tennis court, formal flower gardens and 25 acres of lawn and woodland and you have Hillcrest in the days of its glory.

In that lavish setting, Frances Wolcott, born to high society in Buffalo, entertained lavishly. Her guest list might be called a cross section of "Who's Who" in the America of the early 1900s.

On the list were the millionaire, August Belmont of New York, and his bride-to-be, Eleanor Robson, the lovely actress.

Mrs. Wolcott's team of chestnuts with white manes and in tan harness to match her carriage of natural wood, was a familiar sight in York. In the early 1900s, one day the carriage swept up to the combination postoffice–general store and from it stepped a stranger. Her personality was as vivid as her costume—a red cape and hood.

That was Ethel Barrymore's first appearance in little York. She came to visit Mrs. Wolcott several times in later years and autographed pictures of the "queen of the stage's royal family" adorned many Hillcrest rooms.

On the grand piano in the central room once stood the head, in bronze, of another First Lady of the stage, Katharine Cornell. She and Mrs. Wolcott were fellow natives of Buffalo and close friends.

Another guest at Hillcrest was Karl Bitter, an eminent

sculptor. He did a life-size profile in medium relief of Edward Knox, born in slavery, who was for years caretaker of the estate. Bitter used as a model another Hillcrest resident, an imported Brown Swiss Bull.

Older Yorkers remember when in 1904 Mrs. Wolcott converted the vast cow barn into a theater and some stage stars appeared in a grand theatrical, in probably the strangest setting in which they had ever displayed their talents. An equally grand reception followed. The rural neighbors for miles around were invited to the barn show but only house guests and the landed gentry of the Valley attended the reception.

The spectacle was a welcome home from their honeymoon in Europe to Mrs. Wolcott's son, Lyman M. Bass, and his bride. Bass was a son of the Lyman Bass who was once Grover Cleveland's Buffalo law partner. His widow married Senator Wolcott.

After Mrs. Wolcott's death, the Basses took over Hillcrest. They maintained it in all its immaculate distinction but its days of splendid entertaining were over.

In 1947 a Rochester woman bought the property and aimed to make Hillcrest a haven for tourists. Because of poor health, she sold it in 1964 to a Caledonia man, who runs a liquor store in the grand house where in another era Teddy Roosevelt and Ethel Barrymore had been among the (non-paying) guests.

So the glory that was Hillcrest's has departed. Those gracious days are as dead as are most of the notables who visited there. As this is written, Alice Roosevelt Long-

118

worth is living in Washington, her tongue growing sharper with the years.

* * *

"Old Brick School 8" stands—but not sturdily—at York Four Corners, a little back from the main street. It began life as a temple of learning, then became in succession, a dwelling, a storage place for town highway machinery and finally, a vacant historical landmark.

Chester Alan Arthur, our 21st and most dandified President, was only seven when he began his schooling in that old building. He was a sturdy, dark-eyed boy with pleasant manners. His father was the Rev. William Arthur, who, like most Baptist preachers of the times, moved from place to place.

Chester was born in 1830 in Fairfield, Vt. Two years later the family moved to the village of Perry in Wyoming County. "Elder" Arthur served the Baptists in that Western New York community for five years and the white house in which baby Chester played still stands on Perry's Elm Street.

In 1837 Preacher Arthur accepted a call from the Baptist church in nearby York. There he found many settlers of his own Scotch-Irish blood. The little house in which the family lived has been gone many years from the York Landing Road. The church in which the father of a President preached burned in 1909.

Local histories insist that the Arthurs lived in York until 1842. President Arthur's biographer, George F. Howe, has

119

the family moving to Union Village near Saratoga Springs, in 1839. In the little cemetery at "the Forks," just outside York village, is a plain marble slab with this inscription:

George, Son of William and Malvina Arthur
Born in 1836. Died in March 1839.

That proves only that the Arthurs were in York in the Spring of 1839. They came there in 1837 and even a Baptist preacher usually stayed more than two years in a place.

The Arthur biography relates this incident of Chester Arthur's boyhood which reveals a trait which characterized his future course as a politician:

"When Chester was a boy, you might see him in the village street after a shower, watching other boys build a mud dam across the rivulet in the roadway. Pretty soon he would be ordering one boy to bring stones, another sticks and others sod to finish the dam. His orders were given in such a way that all did his bidding without question. But he took care not to get any of the dirt on his own hands."

Chester Arthur, educated at Union College, was state quartermaster general during the Civil War. He became a successful lawyer in New York City and second in command of Roscoe Conkling's Republican "Stalwart" machine. The Blaine faction called Arthur "the spoilsman boss of the customs house."

After James A. Garfield emerged from the deadlocked convention of 1880 as the compromise candidate, Arthur was named as his running mate to appease Conkling.

Garfield had served only a few months before he was fatally wounded by a demented office seeker.

In the White House, Chester A. Arthur rose above partisanism and machine politics. He had associated with the spoilsmen but "took care not to get any of the dirt on his own hands." He was a cultivated, well read, fastidious gentleman who played politics as a fascinating game.

President Arthur pushed Civil Service reform, an investigation of postal frauds and took other steps that pained his former Stalwart friends.

The tall portly man in the frock coat and with the magnificent burnsides, who first conned his lessons in a district schoolhouse in rural York, was by no means the least able of our Presidents.

* * *

There's a plot of land in the Town of Wayne which belongs to the President of the United States. It has since 1868.

The deed is recorded in the Steuben County Clerk's office at Bath. In it, on Nov. 16, 1868, Moses Crookston conveyed "to the President of the United States, because of my natural love and affection for my family, the property herein described, four rods square, in the Town of Wayne, reserving there the right to burial for myself and wife and to be held as a burial place for my children."

A Johnson was in the White House in 1868. Then it was Andrew. There is no reason to believe that any President, including and since Andy Johnson, has known that he had title, during term of office, to a private cemetery near Keuka Lake in Upstate New York.

Crookston's motive is a mystery. Perhaps he sought to insure perpetual care of his burial plot by deeding it to the President. If so, his hope was a vain one.

I would never have found "the President's land" had it not been for Alderman F. Gleason whose farm and vineyards are on the east side of Keuka Lake on land his ancestors tilled in the early years of settlement. Gleason remembered the private cemetery and offered to take me to it although he had not seen it in years.

He found the site just off the road. It is a veritable jungle in which stands the well-hidden 11-foot marble obelisk with a stone base, surrounded by an ornate iron fence.

On the monument are the names of "Moses Crookston, who died Jan. 23, 1878, aged 72" and "his wife, Sarah, who died Nov. 15, 1868, aged 70 years." On the shaft is this epitaph:

"Our parents—
Our father and mother are gone;
They lay beneath the sod.
Dear parents, although we miss you much,
We know you rest with God."

No other Crookstons are buried there.

It's high time that the President of the United States

clears the land he owns in the Town of Wayne, County of Steuben.

* * *

A President of the United States once was motorman of a Rochester trolley car—for a few blocks.

The temporary motorman was the bearded, dignified Hoosier Republican, Benjamin Harrison, and the date was Sunday, May 29, 1892. He came to Rochester to dedicate the Soldiers and Sailors Monument in Washington Square, a ceremony watched by thousands the next day, Memorial Day.

Many other notables came for the long-awaited unveiling of the Civil War memorial, which is crowned by the brooding figure of Lincoln. Among them was Roswell P. Flower, the millionaire Democratic Governor of New York.

On Sunday the Presidential party rode to Charlotte for breakfast at the Cottage Hotel and was returning to the downtown section in the "palace car" of the local street railways when Harrison was asked to "play motorman." The regular man on the throttle, you may be sure, kept a close watch on his substitute's performance.

The car had traveled a short distance south on Lake Avenue when John N. Beckley, president of the railways, noticed Bishop Bernard J. McQuaid of the Rochester Roman Catholic diocese, standing along the track.

The trolley was stopped (not by "Motorman" Harrison,

123

according to any report of the incident) and Bishop Mc-
Quaid was invited aboard.

Governor Flower took the place of the President at the
controls and the Presbyterian Harrison sat beside the
Catholic bishop. The two were engaged in animated conversation during the rest of the trip.

Chapter 15

John L. Sullivan vs John Barleycorn

For hours the lobby and bar of the Livingston House on Rochester's Exchange Street have been filled with cigar-smoking men in derby hats. Nearly all the sporting fraternity of the city is there. The air that hot July afternoon is tense with expectancy.

"Where's the champ? Where's John L.?" men ask each other as the twilight shadows fall. They watch the door for the sight of a familiar figure, a giant, barrel-chested, ham-handed, hazel-eyed, gaudily garbed Irishman and the roar of a familiar voice:

"My name is John L. Sullivan and I can lick any . . . . in the world. And the drinks are on me."

The date is July 2, 1889 and "the battle of the century" is only six days away. "Somewhere near New Orleans" John Lawrence Sullivan, the Boston Strong Boy, is to defend his heavyweight boxing title against Jake Kilrain.

The newspapers had announced that Sullivan was to arrive in Rochester that afternoon from his training camp at Belfast, a Genesee River village some 70 miles to the southward, and that he probably would stop at the Livingston before boarding his special train for the Southern battle site.

The waiting crowd knows that the special is in the New York Central yards, steam up. It knows, too, that a morning train had brought to town a delegation of wise-eyed New Yorkers, their pockets full of bills, and that among them are Sullivan's backers, Jimmy Wakeley and Charley Johnson, who are to accompany the champ to the bout.

But no John L. shows up at the Livingston House. His special train pulls out without him.

His fans at the hotel are perplexed. It is not like John L. to give waiting admirers the slip. It had not been that way at all when the champ came to Rochester in 1882 on a barnstorming tour. John L. liked people. He was never one to dodge crowds.

Later it is learned that Sullivan came to town from Belfast on the Olean branch of the Pennsylvania Railroad, got off at the West Main Street station, hopped into a carriage, was driven to Chili, whence he walked the dirt road to Churchville, where the special train picked him up. Why the secrecy?

The answer was Billy Muldoon, his trainer for the past three months. In the puritanical code of that Irishman with the icy blue eyes and the unbending will, visits to bars by a defending champion on the eve of a crucial fight had no part.

William Muldon had hardly let the irresponsible, dram-loving John L. out of his sight during the rigorous training

period in Belfast and he was taking no chances in Rochester.

So the Sullivan Special rolled on to New Orleans. The
rest is an oft-told tale, how to dodge the law, the gladiators
met at Richburg, Miss., and, toe to toe, fought 75 rounds
before, after two hours and 18 minutes of bare knuckle
fighting under the old London rules, the seconds of the
battered Kilrain tossed in the towel.

It had been common knowledge that a few weeks before
the bout John Barleycorn had John L. Sullivan nearly on
the ropes and the sporting world marveled at his comeback. The answer to the "miracle" again was Billy Muldoon.

We must go back a few years to the time when Muldoon,
then wrestling champion of the world, had taken under his
wing a bulking Irish lad from Boston, had clad him in fine
raiment and had given him a chance in the New York
ring.

The Irish lad, who soon became a sensation because of
his stamina, did not stick to Muldoon. He took up other
managers. He went down the glory road, finally to become
world champion. He came to like the taste of champagne,
to keep irregular hours, to go on terrific benders, and
when he was finally induced to fight Kilrain, he was to
quote Muldoon, "a drunken, bloated mass of flesh and
bone without a dollar in his pocket."

But he was still undefeated champion, he still had a
powerful, albeit much abused, body, and he still was the
idol of the multitude.

So Billy Muldoon made a daring proposition to Sullivan's backers, who had bound themselves to a side bet of $10,000 on the Kilrain fight. Muldoon offered to put Sullivan in shape for the championship bout. If John L. won, the ten grand was Muldoon's. If he lost, all his training efforts were wasted. Muldoon insisted upon one thing —that the champion be put under his absolute control.

With his beloved title at stake, John L. would agree to anything. So it came about that in the late Spring of 1889, the wreck of what had been America's finest fighter went to Belfast to train under the most exacting martinet in the world of sports.

It was not by chance that Belfast, an Allegany County farming community in the foothills beside the meandering Genesee, was chosen for the training camp. Billy Muldoon had been born in that countryside. The red-thatched farm boy became known as the strongest lad in those parts.

At 18 he was in the Union Army with Phil Sheridan's Cavalry. After the Civil War, he went to New York, joined the police force, became its best wrestler and eventually the Graeco-Roman wrestling champion of the universe, retiring undefeated.

Muldoon had a taste of stage life, appearing with Maurice Barrymore as Charles the Wrestler in "As You Like It." He was a respected figure in the sports world of 1889. To him the human body was a holy temple and he who profaned it by loose living was a fool. Physical fitness was a fetish with him. This inflexible tyrant became trainer, guardian and veritable jailer of the swashbuckling

128

Sullivan, who loved wine, women and song and detested rules and restraint.

Muldoon had built in the center of Belfast a house with wide porches. There were other buildings, a training stable, a carriage house, employees' quarters and eventually a bowling alley.

Belfast, then as now, had fewer than 1,000 inhabitants. Across the street from the Muldoon property was the Catholic church and cemetery and the Protestant burying ground was nearby. It was a quiet place, the most tranquil that John L., who reveled in the bright lights, had ever known.

Sullivan ordered his extensive wardrobe shipped to Belfast. Muldoon countermanded the order. Fancy clothes did not fit into his training system.

That was the beginning of an epic clash of wills between the two strong Irishmen which has given rise to countless stories and legends that still live in the river towns.

Belfast had one hotel and one saloon. Muldoon forbade the owners of both to sell John L. Sullivan a drink. He banned all reporters from the camp, with one exception, Ban Johnson, who was to organize and head the American Baseball League. Muldoon trusted him. He wanted no out-of-town visitors around. So he engaged every room in the hotel. He also asked the villagers to keep away from his charge.

Under such restrictions, Sullivan, a sick man because of his debauches, began the most severe training any boxer up to that time had ever known. Muldoon hardly let him out of his sight. He even slept on a cot beside him at night.

Soon the regular hours, country air, wholesome food and abstemious living began to bear fruit. The fighter had a superb constitution in his favor.

From morn to night the relentless Muldoon put his man through the paces—dumb bell exercises, gruelling road work, wrestling, bag punching, tossing a medicine ball (a Muldoon creation), rope skipping. Muldoon was a pioneer in this type of training.

The high spirited Sullivan rebelled. Muldoon would not yield an inch. For two days the two men never spoke to each other. John L. was the first to give ground. When the day for the big fight drew near, Billy knew his work had been good. It was a far different champion who left Belfast July 2 than the sodden wreck who had landed there a few months before.

Charles Van Every's biography of Muldoon, "The Solid Man of Sport," pictures the road work at Belfast as seen through the eyes of Ban Johnson.

Muldoon, stalking grimly ahead, would set the pace for Sullivan's morning workout over eight miles of country road. Twenty-five feet behind his trainer trotted John L., roughly clad and gripping a blackthorn stick, with Mike Cleary, assistant trainer, at his side. Three dogs brought up the rear. Friends and well wishers who wanted to accompany the champ were brusquely shooed away by Muldoon. He kept Sullivan at this grind day after day.

Old timers around Belfast claim Muldoon sometimes

drove a team hitched to a buckboard on these hikes, with the champion trotting behind. The route followed a road east of the river, thence to Caneadea, where there was a tavern. There John L. was allowed one glass of beer—and only one. Then the retinue returned to camp via the main road through Oramel.

Van Every relates that once Sullivan broke loose from his jailer and reached the village's only saloon where he cowed the proprietor into serving him drinks. As was his wont, he bought for all hands in the place.

Muldoon heard of it and came on the run. With one sweep of his brawny arm, he cleared the bar of the round of drinks and gave the saloon keeper the tongue lashing of his life. Meanwhile John L. had fled. Muldoon knew where to find him—at the only other bar in town. There Sullivan had cowed the hotel keeper into pouring him a drink when Muldoon burst in. The "Solid Man" tossed $25 on the bar and told the hotel man to close it up for the night.

John L. made a try for more booze at the drug store but the druggist, fearing Muldoon more than the big fighter, turned him away. When the "Strong Boy" returned to the white house, the two Irishmen had it out. In effect Muldoon told his charge: "One more break like that and I am through and you lose your title." That sobered Sullivan.

Local legend has it that John L. eluded his jailer more than once and on such occasions, the cry would go up in Belfast's quiet streets: "John L. is loose again. Send for Muldoon." Women and children would scurry for cover and the glowering trainer would clatter up to the tavern or saloon, throw Sullivan into the back of the vehicle and cart him back to camp.

Down the river they tell also how Sullivan wired his special girl friend, Ann Livingston, to visit him in Belfast and how Muldoon intercepted the telegram and sent another, commanding Ann to stay away.

Whether it was during one of Sullivan's barnstorming tours or during the Belfast training period, there's a tale that Father Flaherty, Mount Morris' famous unfrocked priest, put on the gloves with John L. and acquitted himself creditably.

For three years after the Sullivan stay, Muldoon maintained his Belfast camp. There he conditioned Kilrain and other sports figures. Mike Cleary came back to the river village to die. Police Superintendent Murray of New York regained his health through the Muldoon method. In 1892 the Solid Man founded his widely known health center near White Plains and abandoned the Belfast enterprise.

He and Sullivan split after the Kilrain scrap and although there was a reconciliation, they were never close again. John L. always stood in awe of his former trainer and looked back on those all-too-quiet Belfast days in retrospective horror.

When John L. died in 1918, Muldoon attended the funeral and tears blurred his frosty blue eyes at the grave. Perhaps he was thinking of the young fellow from Boston he had first known so long ago.

Muldoon, who late in life became a member of the New

York State Athletic Commission, gave his property in Belfast to the Catholic Church. The house where Sullivan had slept was used as a home for nuns and to this day is called the Convent House. Most of its porches are gone. Until a few years ago in the former training stable two iron rings on which once John L. swung were still hanging from the ceiling.

Few are left who remember when the peace of the village was broken by the cry:

"John L. is loose again. Send for Muldoon!"

Chapter 16

Uncle Grover Stole the Show

The Time: High Noon of June 10, 1891.

The Place: A Victorian house under tall trees on High Street in Walworth village.

The principal characters, by all the rules, should have been two bright-eyed sisters, cool and lovely in their white silk gowns and each carrying a bouquet of June roses. For it was their wedding day and they were of the upper crust of the countryside, members of a family long prominent in the social, political and business life of the community.

The double wedding had drawn to the house on the hill some 100 guests. And of course, there were the two bridegrooms, both dashing young Westerners.

Strange to say, the center of attention was none of these. It was a fat and taciturn middle-aged man with a bull neck and a generous mustache. His ponderous frame was swathed in a frock coat. It was a blistering hot day and he sweated profusely. The saw-like edges of his wing collar clawed at his several chins. He was an uncomfortable figure and hardly a prepossessing one. Yet he stole the

134

show at one of Wayne County's most brilliant social affairs.

The burly, perspiring wedding guest was Grover Cleveland, who already had served one term as President and who the next year was to stage an unprecedented comeback and wrest from Benjamin Harrison the office he had lost in 1888 to the Hoosier Republican. The two brides were Cleveland's nieces, Nellie and Anna, daughters of his sister, Susan, who was the wife of the Hon. Lucien Theron Yeomans, of Walworth's "First Family."

The presence of a former President of the United States in a quiet, off-the-beaten-path Wayne County village needs some explaining.

To Walworth, which began life in 1801 as Douglas Corners, there came from Eastern New York in the 1830s one Theron Gilbert Yeomans, then in his teens. He became a wealthy and influential citizen, a sort of Walworth grandee.

He operated a large nursery business, went into fruit growing on a large scale and brought a new variety of pear from France to Western New York. He imported Holstein-Friesian cattle to augment his thoroughbred herd. He once owned a cow that produced more butter in a single year than any bovine had ever produced before.

Theron Yeomans traveled extensively, in the United States and abroad. He was a local power in politics and served in the State Assembly. He was a delegate to the G.O.P. national convention of 1884 that nominated James G. Blaine as its standard bearer. Blaine's successful Democratic opponent was Grover Cleveland. Yeomans was a

135

temperance man and built the Pacific Hotel, which sold no booze. The building still stands in the village and houses stores.

Theron's son, Lucien, became associated with his father's many enterprises. He, too, was elected to the Assembly. The Yeomans family built handsome homes. Albert, nephew of Theron, once was sheriff of the county.

In 1865 a smart and determined young woman named Susan Cleveland came to Walworth as preceptress of the Academy. This daughter of an impecunious minister, one of 10 children, met the son of the wealthy Theron Yeomans. He proposed, and so the story goes, she told him to listen for the school bell. If it rang at a certain hour, her answer was "yes." The bell rang at the appointed time. Wedding bells followed. Lucien and Susan were married in 1867.

Meanwhile, Susan's brother, Grover, was fighting his way up in the law and in politics in the roaring lake front city of Buffalo, and becoming, by virtue of his stubborn, rugged honesty, in turn sheriff, mayor, governor of New York and finally President. It was he who said "public office is a public trust."

Two daughters of the Lucien Yeomans, Nellie and her younger sister, Anna, went West. Nellie studied art in Toledo and there met her future husband, Charles Hamilton. Anna taught school in Beatrice, Neb. and fell in love with Joseph A. Reed of that prairie town.

The sisters decided on a double wedding in their old home and set the day for June 10, 1891.

136

So it came to pass that a former President clambered off a New York Central train at Palmyra that June morning. Grover Cleveland had been in Walworth before. He had gone far since then, with a term in the White House and, after his defeat by Harrison, lush years of corporation law practice in New York. He gained in girth and in conservatism. He had hobnobbed with the great but remained a forthright, unpretentious man with little gift for small talk.

Cleveland had attended another wedding only five years earlier, his own, to the handsome young Frances Folsom in the White House. His bride did not accompany him to Walworth for the double wedding. She was "expecting."

The livery rig of William Bump carried the former President to Walworth from the Palmyra station and back again. To shield his famous brother-in-law from the curious, Lucien Yeomans arranged a little deception. Fritz Seibert of Toledo, best man for Charles Hamilton, was about the same size as Cleveland and Yeomans took Fritz to and from the station in his buggy. Seibert got a kick out of posing as Cleveland and bowed and doffed his hat to many people who thought they were gazing at the ex-President.

A faded clipping tells of the double wedding at high noon "under an arch of smilax, festooned with a horseshoe of white roses." It relates how the fair-haired Nellie entered on the arm of her father with brunette sister Anna following, escorted by her Uncle Grover.

The Rev. William N. Cleveland of Chaumont, an uncle of the brides, performed the ceremony. The clipping ran the long list of guests, some of them from Rochester and told of "two elegant traveling clocks from Tiffany's in New York, the gifts of Mr. and Mrs. Grover Cleveland and the two $100 checks presented by the Hon. Theron G. Yeomans." Caterer Ridley of Newark served a "sumptuous repast."

Between the lines one conjures up the picture of a burly man in stifling rooms, full of Republicans and in a temperance household to boot. Cleveland was fond of his sister and her children but he was never at ease at social functions.

He liked the feel of a fierce tug of a fighting fish on his line; the thrill of his gunfire bringing down a high-flying wild duck, and after the day's sport, a hard fought poker game with his cronies "with a stein upon the table and the good song ringing clear." Grover Cleveland was a man's man. He was no toper, no boor, but he was essentially modest and at Walworth that wedding day everybody wanted to talk to him.

The old house, no longer in the hands of the Yeomans clan, still stands but only a few oldsters remember the glory that descended upon it one June day when a former and future President "stole the show" at the wedding of his two nieces, back in 1891.

In fancy one sees again the frock-coated Falstaffian figure climbing into Will Bump's livery buggy as Grover Cleveland departs for "somewhere east of Walworth, where there are deserving Democrats and a man can quench a thirst."

138

Chapter 17

The Man Who Stole a Train

He was Western New York's Billy the Kid.

The James boys and the Daltons hunted in packs. But Oliver Curtis Perry, specialist in train robbery, always played a lone, bold hand.

He did not look the part. He might have passed for a village apothecary who taught a Bible class on Sundays. He was soft of voice and mild of manner. His brown eyes were disarmingly gentle but when he was trapped, they blazed in fury. His slender, supple figure was clad in sober black and he always wore gloves.

Oliver Curtis Perry will live in criminal annals as the man, who, fleeing a thwarted train robbery, stole an engine and from its cab fought a running gun duel with the crew of a locomotive in pursuit on another track.

The dawn which broke over the frozen Wayne County flats on February 22, 1892, unfolded a strange spectacle—two engines racing, alternately straightaway on parallel tracks, then reversing their paths in the chase, all to the accompaniment of gunfire.

139

They caught Oliver Curtis Perry eventually, but not in his stolen engine. And his career in prison was every bit as fantastic as had been his days of freedom.

The late Emil Laas of Rochester was the last survivor of the train crew which had such a thrilling encounter with Perry in 1892. Then he was the youngest conductor on the division and he walked with a jaunty step as he checked No. 31, a ten-car, all-express train, before it left the New York Central Station in Syracuse.

On the platform he noticed a young man with glasses and a sandy mustache, a bag slung over his shoulder. Something about the young man rang a warning bell in Laas' mind and he cautioned his trainman against allowing anyone near the express cars.

For 31 was hauling a rich cargo. Just ahead of the day coach, where the conductor and trainman rode at the rear of the train, was the money car. There the messenger, young Daniel T. McInerney of Rochester, guarded more than a quarter million dollars.

At Jordan, a few miles out of Syracuse, the conductor heard a hissing sound. He went to the money car and peered through the cord hole. At first a flickering light led him to believe the car was on fire.

Then he saw a stranger pawing over envelopes. Laas yanked the emergency cord. He hopped back into the coach and slammed on the emergency brakes. Before the train ground to a full stop, from the side door of the money car, a gun barked twice and a low voice, full of deadly menace, spoke:

"Get this train to running again or I will blow you all to pieces."

Oliver Curtis Perry, the soft-spoken bandit, had taken over Express Train 31.

Facing two revolvers, Laas had no recourse but to signal the train to start. He slid back into his coach, armed himself with a wrench and waited. At Port Byron came the break he wanted. As the express train thundered into the station, a fast freight stood waiting on another track. Some of its crew were on the platform.

Laas leaped for the emergency brake and pulled with all his strength. Slowly the long train came to a halt. The crew rushed to the money car. There they found the messenger semi-conscious with three bullet wounds in his body. Envelopes and papers were strewn over the floor but the treasure was intact.

There was no bandit in sight. The crew searched the train and concluded that he had fled in the darkness when the train stopped. Laas ordered the train to speed to Lyons after sending a message ahead, telling of McInerney's injuries.

A thrilling game of guns and wits had been played in that money car.

The youth with the glasses and the bag over his shoulder had concealed himself between two cars when the train pulled out of Syracuse. Then he perched atop the money car in the cold until No. 31 reached Jordan.

Out of his bag he took an ingeniously devised rope ladder, with hooks that fitted over the side of the cornice of the car. Carefully he lowered himself to the window. With his revolver butt he smashed the pane.

Dan McInerney was sitting in front of a safe, sorting packages by the light of a kerosene lamp when the crash of glass startled him. He saw a man's head, hidden, except for the eyes, by a red flannel mask, framed in the broken window.

The messenger reached for his gun. He and the bandit fired almost simultaneously. Perry's bullet hit McInerney in the hand. The messenger tried to pull the emergency cord. Perry fired again and wounded McInerney just above his left eyebrow.

Game to the core, the messenger, before he sank to the floor, kicked the chimney off the lamp, plunging the car into darkness. Then Perry reached in and, unloosening the catch, let himself into the car.

For a time the express man was unconscious. The cool breeze coming from the broken window revived him. He pulled the emergency cord feebly. That was the hissing sound Laas had heard. The bandit then touched a match to some waybills. That was the flickering light Laas had seen.

After the messenger again pulled the rope, Perry fired. A wound in the thigh sent the defender of the money car to the floor again. McInerney contrived to sit on a pile of valuable packages and, on orders from Perry, opened some envelopes. Purposely he picked some that contained papers of no value.

It was then that the train was stopped and Perry forced

the crew to proceed. At Port Byron he apparently got off during the search for him, then swung back on as the train resumed its course. Before he left the money car, he bade the messenger a polite "good bye."

At Lyons, where word of the holdup and the wounding of the messenger had been received, a crowd had gathered despite the early hour.

McInerney was lifted from the treasure car he had defended so bravely and was taken to a doctor. Laas hurried into the Lyons station to file a report and spread the alarm. On returning to the train, he saw, coolly mingling in the crowd, the same man he had spotted at Syracuse. Telling the brakeman to "keep an eye on that fellow," he went in search of a policeman.

The brakeman could not wait. He and another railroader made a grab for the sandy youth with the glasses. Pronto they looked into the muzzles of two revolvers.

Perry dashed to the locomotive and tried to detach it from the express train. The automatic coupler balked him. Then he ran across two tracks and pulled the pin from the coupling of a freight engine. Waving his guns, he drove the engineer and fireman from the cab. He climbed in and opened the throttle wide.

As the bandit started the engine, someone in the crowd produced a shotgun. Armed with this weapon, railroad men uncoupled the express locomotive, manned the cab and sped down the tracks in pursuit of the other engine.

When Perry saw the faster locomotive bearing down upon him on a parallel track, he threw his engine into reverse. As the pursuers flashed by, he and the railroaders blazed away at each other. The forces of law and order reversed and caught up with the bandit. They fired and then dropped flat as their antagonist's fire raked their cab. During the chase, Perry blew the whistle at each crossing as if on a routine run.

Several times this maneuver was repeated. The bandit seemed to have plenty of ammunition and he knew how to manipulate a railroad engine. Finally the posse decided to give up the chase and roared back to Lyons for reinforcements.

They did not know that, because of the untended fires in the stolen engine, its steam was running low. Perry saw that he must abandon the vehicle of flight which had stood him in such good stead.

At "the Blue Cut," the robber left the cab and with his guns "persuaded" a switchman he found there to run the engine back to Lyons. Then after it had disappeared down the tracks, Perry set off across the fields on foot, seeking new means of escape.

He demanded and obtained a horse at the nearest house, telling the farmer he was a Pinkerton detective on the trail of a train robber. His shooting irons, one in each gloved hand, were convincing.

After five miles, his mount, a plodding plow horse, tired and Perry decided to switch horses. At another house, a farmer was just hitching a horse to a cutter.

The fugitive repeated his Pinkerton detective story and when the farmer demurred, a shot fired in the air dispelled his doubts. Perry drove away in a horse-drawn cutter, sleigh bells jingling.

He wandered off the main road and found himself on a logging trail which ended in a swamp. Abandoning the horse and cutter, Perry figured he would hide out there. He knew the countryside would be mobilizing.

The farm owner had piled some stones at the edge of the swamp. The outlaw found more and added them to the heap until he had a "fort" about a foot and a half high.

Behind this makeshift redoubt, Oliver Curtis Perry crouched in the snow and waited the course of events.

He did not have long to wait.

As word of the train robbery attempt spread a manhunt was organized under the command of Wayne County Sheriff Thornton. The posse of 30 men was split into groups of five.

One quintet was led by Jeremiah Collins, then a young deputy sheriff. That group set out in a sleigh and came upon the bandit's trail near Benton's Swamp in the Town of Arcadia. Collins was prepared for a fight to the finish with a resourceful criminal.

The lawmen wallowed through the snow until they came to a low stone wall. Collins was in the lead when he heard a shout from the rear.

"Look out, Jerry, he's going to shoot."

From behind the stone pile, a man had risen. His right hand clutched a revolver. "Did I kill that messenger?" he demanded.

Informed that McInerney was alive, the fugitive seemed

145

relieved and began parleying with Collins. First he stipulated that the deputy face him unarmed. Collins replied that he had no gun. He told the bandit he might as well give up, that he faced hopeless odds.

For several minutes the two talked. Jerry Collins was stalling for time. Some of his men were stealing around to the rear of the robber. The hunted man saw the movement and his glance shifted for a second from Collins.

Quick as light, the deputy was upon him, grabbing the bandit around the waist before Perry could move. Down in the snow went the pair in a struggling heap. The posse closed in and a notorious criminal was a prisoner.

He made no attempt to deny his identity. He had left his red mask and rope ladder in the cab of the stolen engine but he still had three guns and ten cartridges.

The bandit who was led back to the Lyons jail was only 27 but he had packed a lot of crime into that short span of years.

He was a native of Fulton County and came from pioneer Yankee stock. At the time of his capture his father was a hard-working carpenter in Syracuse.

When Oliver was 14, he was sent to a state reformatory for burglary. Three years later he repeated the offense and became an inmate of the old red brick Monroe County Penitentiary. There he attacked a guard in a vain attempt at escape.

Shipped off to Minnesota to live with an uncle he robbed his uncle's store, was caught and went to Stillwater Prison for three years. On his release he became a cow

146

hand in Montana. On the range he learned to draw fast and shoot straight. In the West he took his first lessons in train robbery.

Returning East, he worked for a time in Albany railroad shops. It was there he learned how to run a locomotive.

Between holdups and burglaries, he raised money by imposing upon religious people. He was suave and glib and obtained funds to "start all over again" by telling credulous folk he had reformed.

But Oliver Curtis Perry slipped up in his biggest job, robbing the railroad express car with its treasure cargo—thanks to the bravery of a messenger.

In the Lyons jail Perry was kept under tight guard. His trial drew crowds from a wide area. Supreme Court Justice William Rumsey, magnificent in lambrequin whiskers, presided. The prosecutor was S. Nelson Sawyer of Palmyra, who later became a Supreme Court justice.

The trial was brief. Perry pleaded guilty to all four counts of the indictment, asking that the $300 cash found on him and his private arsenal not be confiscated. They were. The sentence was 49 years and three months in state prison.

Perry came face to face in the Court House with Dan McInerney for the first time since their duel in the money car. The bandit said with a smile: "McInerney, you are a brave man. I am sorry I had to shoot you."

When Perry was being taken in irons from Lyons jail to the train bound for Auburn Prison, 2,000 people milled

147

about him. For once he lost his urbanity and snarled at them:

"What do you think I am, some kind of a wild beast? Why in hell do you crowd around me so I can hardly breathe?"

That afternoon the gates of the grim gray prison clanged and Oliver Curtis Perry was shut away from the outside world.

His erratic conduct at Auburn caused him to be adjudged insane and in 1905 he was transferred to Matteawan. He had not been there long before he escaped, with three other prisoners. They made a key out of a spoon that had been smuggled in to them, overpowered a guard and fled over a rooftop.

All were recaptured. Perry was nabbed in the railroad yards at Weehawken, N.J. He seemingly could not keep away from trains.

Soon after his return to Matteawan, Perry made the news again—with a horrifying act. He blinded himself for life in his cell by dropping hot needle points into his eyes.

He was shifted to Dannemora, the North Country "Siberia" of state prisons, and his behavior was sensational indeed. He went on a hunger strike and was forcibly fed for four years. He appealed to the authorities for better food, "not only for myself but all the prisoners." He tore his prison suit to shreds and refused to wear a stitch of outer clothing until he was furnished "a suit of respectable cut."

Reporters interviewed Perry in his cell. They found him in the pink, despite his fasting. The newspapers ran stories

148

about this strange blind man with a white bandage over his eyes, on his cot, his blanket his only raiment.

Perry expressed regret he had blinded himself, saying he did it while under the influence of opium which deadened the pain. He said his family had disowned him and that he hoped his mad act would bring them to his aid. They paid him no attention but some clergymen and reformers became interested in his case.

In 1917 he dictated a long and moving appeal to Governor Whitman, asking for commutation of sentence. He pointed out that he had never murdered anyone, and that he already had served 25 years of a long sentence.

His plea wound up with these words: "My simple prayer is that my sentence be reduced. Otherwise I will have to live among maniacs for 24 more long, dreary years. I pray that the Honorable Governor may lighten my blinded life a little."

This document was taken down by a prison attendant just as Perry had dictated it, even to punctuation marks.

But the "Honorable Governor" could do nothing about it, had he so chosen, for the doctors had pronounced Oliver Curtis Perry incurably insane.

He was 65 when death came to him in the darkness of Dannemora's madhouse. Thirty-seven of his years had been spent in prison, 25 of them in a self-induced world of shadows.

His proud boast had been: "Nobody ever robbed a train just the way I did."

It is doubtful if anybody has since.

Chapter 18

Specks in the Sky

'Twas a balmy Summer afternoon and a goodly crowd was there.

This has nothing to do with the oft-quoted verse about "Joe's barroom on the corner of the square."

Rather this has to do with "The Speck in the Sky" and a carnival, or maybe a county fair, a Fourth of July or Labor Day celebration or Old Home Week.

High carnival is in the air. The crowd has enjoyed the ball game, the foot races, the tug of war and the capture of the greased pig. It even listened—briefly—to the orator of the day. It kept time to the band music.

It has stuck around for the grand finale of the doings, the balloon ascension and the parachute jump. That was the event which stood out in the boldest type on the posters which for weeks had adorned poles, fences and meeting house sheds.

The trench has been dug. The bonfire has been built and is roaring merrily. Over it the big balloon fills slowly with hot air. A shouted "Let'er go, boys," and the men at

150

5. Midway at Charlotte's Amusement Park

6. Long Excursion Trains at Lakeside

the guy ropes let go. The big bag rises until it is up 2,000 feet or more.

Suddenly the watchers become tense. They see a speck dangling from that bag in the sky. The parachutist has cut loose. Down floats the "speck" until it comes into closer view as a human figure under an open "umbrella." It lands easily and with a bow and a flourish acknowledges the plaudits of the crowd.

Another "Flying Allen" has won a brush with death and given another crowd a thrill.

For more than three quarters of a century that scene was repeated countless times. Three generations of "Flying Allens" have thrilled the multitudes at fairs and other events. They rate the title of Western New York's No. 1 family of daredevils.

Grandpa and Grandma thrilled to the stunts of three pioneering Allen brothers in horse and buggy days. Dad and mother chugged out to the fair grounds to see the second generation of Allens perform. The new streamlined age brought a third generation of daredevils, a young generation sadly stalked by tragedy, and with Allen women in the act for the first time.

The act has always been in the blood of the Allen clan. Fear is not in its lexicon. One of them jumped in total darkness. He was blind. Another made a farewell performance at the age of 68.

They have jumped singly and in twos and threes. They have been shot from cannons. They have landed on treetops and on mountains. They have been flung against the sides of buildings. They have been burned when balloons caught fire. Always they have laughed in the face of danger.

They have not always cheated the dark angel that lurks in the shadows for every daredevil. Within a span of 15 years four Allens, two of them girls, lost their lives carrying on the family tradition. Another, a mere boy, was indirectly its victim.

The story of the "Flying Allens" begins in 1875 in the home town of the clan, Dansville, nestling in the shadow of great hills. The pioneers were three brothers, Ira, Comfort and Martin. They liked to do hair-raising stunts when they were schoolboys.

Ira, the eldest, launched the tribe in the public entertainment field in 1875 when he walked a tight rope he had stretched across the old Genesee Valley Canal in Dansville.

Two years later, Martin made his first jump from a balloon at the height of 2,500 feet at the same spot. The brothers had first sent up to 1,000 feet a trial balloon carrying a sand bag of a weight equalling that of a man.

In the early days the Allens did not always use parachutes. They came down with the balloon, hanging on to the trapeze bar at the bottom of the bag. Once Ira landed on a hilltop near Canaseraga, more than 10 miles from his starting point.

The fame of the Allens spread. For years they toured fairs and carnivals, singly, in pairs or as a trio. They varied their balloon act with other stunts. Ira rode a bicycle on a tight rope. He and Martin did double trapeze performances. Faded newspaper clippings tell of their feats.

In later years Martin usually played a lone hand. He collected rattlesnakes and other reptiles and showed them as a side line. He performed on a trapeze bar while his nephew, Warren, Comfort's son, rode a bicycle on a tight wire above his uncle. Comfort did all manner of stunts in his time. In 1896 he collected $900 in prizes at a Providence exhibition.

The three brothers had some close calls but none of them ever was seriously injured. They made their canvas balloons. Comfort had the knack of folding parachutes which accounted in large measure for the Allens' freedom from mishaps.

Ira Allen spent the last 25 years of his long life in darkness. As a teen-ager, he ran away from home to join his father and two older brothers in the Union Army when the Civil War drums beat. He was wounded and eventually became blind as the result of his wounds.

His nephew, Edgar W. "Red" Allen of Dansville, recalls that Ira once jumped after he had lost his sight and that his nephews ran under his balloon, telling the old man where to land. Ira died in 1932 at the age of 86.

Comfort, who in his youth had driven mules on the towpath of the old Genesee Valley Canal, was 80 when he passed away. "Red" maintains that his father many years ago devised an aluminum dirigible but lacked the funds to have it patented.

Martin Allen lived until the age of 90. For years he ran

a jewelry store in Dansville. He made his last jump when he was 68 years old, at a "Booster Day" celebration in the village. The dean of the clan wore his old green tights. He landed safely on East Hill, far above the village.

In their lifetimes the three brothers had often flirted with death. Each died in his bed. Their average life span was 85 years.

Old residents of the area still talk about the time in 1907 when Warren "Speck" Allen, wearing a derby hat, parachuted safely from the 330-foot high Shawmut Railroad bridge in Stony Brook Glen.

He was 29 years old then and already a seasoned performer. He was nicknamed "Speck" because someone, watching one of his jumps from a balloon, said: "Why, he looks like a speck way up there."

The bridge from which "Speck" Allen made his famous leap is gone now and Stony Brook Glen, a scenic showplace of the area, is a state park. The bridge was torn down in 1948 for junk, all 1,267,000 pounds of it, after the Shawmut Railroad, long in receivership, abandoned its 170-mile line that wound over the heights of the Southern Tier and Northern Pennsylvania.

"Speck" Allen made the last of his many jumps, his first in 15 years, in 1938 at Le Roy. He was 62 then. He landed in a cow pasture when his parachute cord became twisted and he was forced to spin around in mid air to untangle it.

He was used to such hazards. Once in Nunda a gust of wind threw him against a tree as he descended and both his legs were broken. And once he was drawn against a Dans-

154

ville building and injured—because somebody failed to loose a guy rope.

Warren, "Speck," who no longer is in the land of the living, became an almost legendary figure around Dansville because of that 1907 leap from the high bridge in Stony Brook Glen.

About that time another Allen, Stephen, son of Martin, was making balloon ascensions. He was seriously injured in Dansville when his balloon caught on telephone wires and he fell 20 feet. Steve Allen died in 1917.

At the time of "Speck's" memorable leap in 1907, his twin brothers, Edgar, "Red," and Edward, were jumping off poles and barns with umbrellas as parachutes. Ed made his debut as a daredevil at the age of 13, his twin the next year, at the Lockport Fair.

Jovial "Red" Allen, operator of a welding business in Dansville and a past district commander of the American Legion (the twins served in World War I) has many tales of his adventures.

In his second year as a performer the ropes became twisted in his descent at a show in Delhi and he could not open the 'chute. However, he landed, unhurt, in the top of a tall pine tree on a mountain five miles from the scene of his takeoff.

And there was the time in Dansville that he escaped banging against a bank building only by pushing himself away from it with his feet. He eventually landed in a roofless garage, under construction. He crashed down amid some scaffolding and got out through a window, with only a few scratches.

For several years the twins did a double jump act. One of their stunts was to eat ice cream cones as they dangled from trapeze bars high above the crowd. Once they had a poodle in the act. The dog jumped with them and had its own red, white and blue parachute which, by means of an ingenious rigging, was loosed as the brothers leaped.

Some animal lovers protested and when the Allens showed up at the Hemlock "World's Fair," the Livingston County sheriff warned them he would stop the act and arrest them for cruelty to animals if the poodle jumped. The twins rigged up a dummy and dropped it, instead of the pooch. The sheriff, thinking the Allens had defied him, came on the run. When he saw the dummy, "he was sore as hell," to quote "Red."

The twins sometimes were billed as "The Devils of the Air." Ed also was called "The Human Comet" and Edgar, as was his father, was dubbed "The Professor."

"Red" Allen will tell you that the wind is always an important figure in parachuting and that a jumper always looks for a big back yard or open field in which to land. He said the jumper can control his 'chute to a certain extent and recalled that in two jumps the same day in Coudersport, Pa., he landed in almost the identical spot each time.

"Red" made his last jump at Byersville near Nunda in 1928, shortly after his marriage. He went up in an old balloon. Its top burst at 300 feet. His 'chute opened just before he hit the ground. His wind was knocked out and so was his jumping career. His wife put her foot down and grounded her Edgar permanently.

After his twin retired, Ed Allen carried on alone until his sons and daughters were old enough to join the act and the panel truck with the legend, "The Flying Allens" on its side became a familiar sight in many states.

Eddie Jr. was 18 when he made his first jump in 1936. He was a tall, sturdy youth, a star athlete at Batavia High School.

The next year, his sisters, Gloria, 17, and Florence, 15, made their debuts in a duo act in Youngstown, Ohio. They were the first feminine Allens to take to the air.

At home in Batavia, a younger brother and still younger sister were eager to join the act as soon as they were old enough. All were trained by that intrepid veteran, their father, Edward Allen, known to intimates as "Bill."

Soon the three personable youngsters, Eddie, Gloria and Florence, billed as the "world's youngest jumpers," were rocketing to national attention. They were a colorful trio, dressed alike in white jodhpurs, dark skirts and white ties, floating down together under their spreading parachutes from the big balloon.

They added a new wrinkle to their act. Two of them were shot from a cannon suspended from the balloon before they parachuted to earth. The stunt was well received.

September, 1937, found the trio, under the management of their father, on a successful Southern tour. On Sept. 23

the Allens were headliners at the Tri-County Fair in Blackstone, Va. That day tragedy struck for the first time in the long history of the clan.

As the three began their descent from a height of 2,000 feet, Gloria's parachute swung against the rigging of brother Eddie's 'chute. It was ripped from skirt to crown. Gamely, Gloria pedaled and maneuvered under the torn parachute to break her fall.

In that fall her young body was crushed. As she was being rushed to a hospital, Gloria begged: "Don't give up the act because I am hurt."

She lost her seven-day fight for life. Hundreds of schoolmates and neighbors attended the funeral services in St. Joseph's Church, Batavia. A memorial stone, the gift of friends in the Virginia town where she died, stands at her grave.

The family heeded Gloria's plea "not to give up the act." Florence and Eddie carried on in 1938 and their cousin, Warren Jr., "Speck's" son, joined them.

On Feb. 19, 1942, tragedy struck the Edward Allens again. Joseph, their 15-year-old son, was a chemically minded freshman at Batavia High School. He was conducting an experiment in the basement of the family home, taking apart a high explosive bomb used in the cannon act. It exploded in his hands. Joseph was injured fatally. He had planned to take his place in the family act the next Summer.

In World War II, Eddie became an officer in the Air

Force. The 100 parachute jumps he had made helped to pay his way through the University of Pennsylvania where he starred in football and wrestling.

Florence married and, as did young Ed, quit the hazardous family business. Warren Jr. remained a "Flying Allen," making jumps in many places in Western New York and Northern Pennsylvania. His wife, Pearl, made occasional jumps with him until 1941.

Early in 1946, Warren, 46 years old and the father of six children, announced his retirement as a stunt man, because it was "too risky for a man with a family." He sold his equipment. He had made 500 jumps.

On July 4, 1946, Warren agreed to make one last flight, at Salamanca. It was to oblige a friend, Buddy Radley, 19-year-old barnstormer who had been hurt, not seriously, when he parachuted into the path of an Erie train.

The Salamanca crowd was horrified when just as Warren's hot air balloon lurched skyward, its undersection ripped away at the seams. The 'chutist clung to the freed trapeze and parachute attachment. He hit the ground from 50 feet in the air. Warren was fatally injured. On his way to the hospital he rallied long enough to implore a grieving Buddy Radley to "quit this business."

At the same time another member of the ill-starred third generation of Allens was carrying the banner. Arlene, the 17-year-old daughter of the Edward Allens, made her fifth balloon ascension at a Bristol, Tenn. carnival on July 27, 1946. It was her last.

Her descending parachute hit a wire charged with 6,600 volts. Her clothing was set afire and her body seared. But she escaped instant death because her body and a metal ring of the parachute rigging hit the high tension wire almost simultaneously. The metal ring caused a short circuit which tripped an automatic switch, shutting off the power.

After Arlene had been four days in an oxygen tent, her recovery seemed certain. She was brought home to Batavia in a bed rigged up in the family's panel truck, the one with the name, "The Flying Allens" on its side. The accident took her young life although she lingered until the Fall of 1948. It was the fourth tragedy in the dauntless family within 15 years.

Her grieving father, Edward B. Allen, a true showman, resolved that "the act must go on." He kept the family banner flying, this last of "the Flying Allens," performing all over the country, until 1965 when a broken leg suffered at a fair in Portland, Conn., finally "grounded" him.

He then was 70 and had made more than 3,000 jumps in 53 years. Allen sold his equipment to a Pennsylvania group which he supervised and trained. Robert Trauger, 29, who took over Allen's act, was killed in September, 1968, when his balloon hit a live wire. That was another tragedy in Ed's life, for he was fond of Trauger.

The genial, broad-shouldered "dean emeritus" of his profession makes his home in Batavia with Mrs. Allen, who accompanied her husband on all his tours. Allen works at the tent and awning business in season. He's spry for his years and misses the thrills that were his for more than half a century.

Through all the years he never lost his sunny smile or his friendly spirit.

Chapter 19

Scholarly Bandit

The hands of the clock in the tall tower on the hill pointed to the hour of 2 A.M. It was the morning of Feb. 14, 1913 and it was bitter cold.

The chilled policeman on his beat stamped his feet as he reached Rochester's windiest corner, Main and St. Paul sts., and surveyed a seemingly deserted downtown.

A rattling and a banging broke the frigid silence and the cop's body tensed. Diagonally across the street from the service elevator exit of the Chamber of Commerce (now the Commerce Building), he saw five overalled figures emerge, each trundling a can of ashes.

The policeman relaxed. "Just the city ash gang," he told himself as he resumed his dreary patrol.

He little knew that he had witnessed the climax of one of the most audacious crimes in Rochester annals; that "the ash gang" was in reality one of the nation's most clever burglary gangs, led by a man who was to rate the title of "master crook," or that along with the ashes, the men in overalls had removed from the Commerce Building some $3,000 worth of jewelry.

162

The haul would have been a quarter of a million had not a safe blower botched his job.

Such was Rochester's introduction to the notorious "Dutch" Anderson, who in later years was often to visit—without felonious intent—the city on the Genesee, which became a sort of "vacation" haven for him.

Few knew of his visits. Who would recognize in the polished, scholarly man who spoke four languages and collected rare books, the leader of one of the most resourceful criminal mobs in the land?

In the Fall of 1912, a smooth-spoken, well dressed man in his early 30s visited the wholesale jewelry establishment of Philip Present in the Chamber of Commerce Building. He represented himself as a dealer from the Middle West who wished to look over the Present stock. He left without buying anything but promised to return. During his visit, he pointed to a large safe and remarked to Present:

"You must have a lot of jewelry in there."

Innocently, the wholesale jeweler answered:

"About a quarter of a million dollars worth."

Afterwards Philip Present recalled the glint that shone in the blue eyes of the supposed dealer, who next he was to meet in a court of justice.

"Dutch" Anderson kept his promise to return to the Present store. For months the vision of the safe which housed a fortune in jewels danced before his eyes.

One night early in February, 1913, five men got off a train at the station in Central Avenue. They had come from Toledo, then a hideout of the criminal world. They spent several days getting "the lay of the land" in Roches-

163

ter. The master mind in their strategy was the quiet, blond, well knit man who spent his spare time searching book stores and libraries for rare volumes.

They chose the morning of Feb. 14 to strike. The cold had driven even the hardiest "night hawks" off the streets and the coast was clear when the five men made their way to the Commerce Building.

First they forced the padlock of the iron gate at the front entrance. Two of them surprised and overpowered the engineer in the basement, tied him up with a clothes line and gagged him. Two others seized the night watchman on his rounds and gave him the same treatment. The fifth acted as lookout.

Then they went to work on the largest of the five safes in the Present store, the one that their leader had marked in his mind for plunder a few months earlier. But their plans went awry. Maybe the "peterman" had had a drop too many. Maybe his mixture of "soup" had been faulty. At any rate a charge of nitroglycerine failed to shatter the inner door. It only moved it off its hinges.

So the gang had to be satisfied with the contents of a salesman's sample trunk full of watch cases, diamonds and other jewelry, with a total value of about $3,000.

Then came the grand getaway scene—the overalls, the ash cans, the basement elevator—that worked perfectly. After the engineer had freed himself and gave the alarm, police were delayed in entering the building because the yeggs had substituted a padlock of their own for the one they had forced on the outside door.

"Dutch" Anderson never bragged about the Present job, despite the success of the "ashcan" camouflage. His men had been clumsy in several ways. One of them dropped a locket, containing the picture of a comely girl. A satchel turned up at the Central Station with other clues—clothing, a time table, another picture of a girl, this one fondling a wooly dog and a cake of soap with the name of a Toledo hotel upon it.

In a few weeks the clues they had left behind led to the arrest of Joseph Hill and Bert Donaldson. They were convicted and given prison terms. The astute Rochester captain of detectives, William H. Whaley, wrung from the pair the identities of their three confederates.

In the Rochester police archives is a circular dated May 22, 1913, signed by Chief of Police Joseph M. Quigley and captioned in large letters: "$200 Reward."

The circular bore pictures and descriptions of the trio still wanted for the Present job. One was Leo Mitchell alias Pope, "a safe blower." Another was James Cordano alias "Gold Tooth Jimmy." The third was given the most prominence. Three pictures of a clean shaven man stretched across the page and under them was this description:

"George Anderson alias George Brown alias Edward Bauer alias Dutch alias the Swede; 32 years old, 5 feet, 7 inches, 156 pounds, blue eyes, fair complexion, medium build."

Anderson used many an alias in his long criminal career.

165

But never on any police circular did his real name appear. That was a secret he guarded all his life.

It was four years before the law caught up with him and he was brought back to face a Monroe County court for his part in the Present theft. He pleaded guilty and drew a five-year sentence to Auburn Prison.

While "Dutch" was in that grim, gray prison over which Copper John has mounted vigil since 1823, he met two men who were to play vital roles in his career.

One was a Rochester lawyer, the late William J. "Big Bill" Baker. Anderson had heard of this massive, affable barrister who was gaining a reputation as a brilliant "mouthpiece" for criminals. He sent for Baker, who thereafter was not only to be "Dutch's" counsel but his trusted confidant.

When he was not being hunted, the gangster made what he called "vacation trips" to Rochester to see his lawyer, Baker. There was an understanding with police that Anderson was to report at headquarters whenever he came to town, give his pledge he would not pull any jobs in the city and in return, the police would let him alone.

And it was in Auburn that "Dutch" first met the flamboyant, trigger-happy Gerald Chapman whose name was to be linked with his as one of the leaders of the shadowy realm of the underworld. The scholarly Anderson had been assigned to teach Spanish classes at the prison school. One of his pupils was the alert-minded, younger Chapman. "Dutch" tutored Chapman in criminal science—on the side.

After Anderson had served his stretch in Auburn, he visited Rochester and called on Detective Capt. John P. McDonald at the old Police Headquarters on Exchange Street. He told "Captain Jack" that henceforth he was "going straight."

A few weeks later the captain read that "Dutch" had been arrested with Chapman in the $2 million holdup of a mail truck in New York City.

Attorney Baker was associated with the defense in the trials that saw Anderson and Chapman sent to Atlanta Federal Prison for long terms. Both escaped—Chapman by shooting his way over the prison wall, Anderson by more subtle means.

"Dutch", who included gardening among his avocations, had charge of the prison rose garden. He slept in a tent nearby. The tools that won him freedom were hidden among the rose bushes he tended with such care.

Their freedom was short lived. Chapman was captured, tried, convicted and doomed to die for the slaying of a policeman.

Anderson, suspected of the killing of a key witness against Chapman in Muncie, Ind., in August, 1925, had to hide out in the Middle West.

On Nov. 2, 1925, two days before Chapman's final plea to escape the death penalty was denied by the Connecticut courts, a Muskegon, Mich. detective named Hammond picked up a well-dressed stranger on suspicion of passing a counterfeit $20 bill.

As the detective was taking his prisoner through an alley

to the police station, little dreaming whom he had in tow, Anderson, knowing his identity would soon be discovered, broke away and ran. There are two versions of what followed.

The press dispatches indicated that the prisoner shot first, mortally wounding his captor, who wrested the criminal's gun from his hand and with his dying breath shot Anderson to death.

Bill Baker, who went to Muskegon to take charge of his client's body, always maintained that Anderson never carried a gun, that the detective shot first and while Hammond was bending over the dying man, "Dutch" grabbed the officer's gun and dispatched him.

The body of one who had been one of the elite of the criminal world lay in a small town morgue all night before it was identified. In police files all over the nation, he was listed as George "Dutch" Anderson with many an alias, specialist in safe blowing, forgery, confidence games, daring holdups, jail breaks and leader of a versatile criminal mob.

George Anderson was not his real name. And the air of distinction and aplomb that clung to him was no veneer. It was by right of birth and breeding.

His real name was Ivan Dahl von Teller and he was born around 1881 in a mansion in Denmark. His family was wealthy and in youth he was given every cultural advantage.

A brilliant student, he was sent to famed Heidelberg University in Germany. After his graduation—without a single saber scar—he returned to Denmark and the repressive influence of his domineering father. He became involved in some boyish scrape and hot words were exchanged between the proud old man and the high spirited youth.

That was the beginning of Ivan Dahl von Teller's long revolt against constituted authority.

At the age of 20 he ran away to America, shed his aristocratic name and became a member of a band of New York crooks. But he never shed the good manners and the love of literature which were instilled in him as a boy in the Old World.

Early in his career of crime, something happened that made him a bitter enemy of society all the rest of his days. Hunted down by bloodhounds in the South for a burglary which he always swore he never committed, he was "railroaded" to a prison turpentine camp where he was frequently lashed and was chained to another convict while at work.

After that his road was clearly charted. He rose to the heights in his chosen "calling," became the leader of a criminal gang and he died ingloriously.

It was only after Anderson's death that the Rochester lawyer, Baker, revealed what he knew of his client's early life. Although Baker had been "Dutch's" trusted friend, he caught only fragmentary glimpses of the gangster's background. Anderson was protecting a proud family name. His relatives were people of consequence in the homeland. A relative was in the diplomatic service.

169

And above all, there was a little old lady in the mansion over the sea, the widowed Madam von Teller, who wrote regularly to "Ivan," the son she thought was a successful businessman in America.

Bill Baker saw to it that she was informed only that her son had died suddenly. He said at the time: "She does not read the American newspapers. She never knew her son's story. Please God, she never shall."

"Dutch" Anderson's antecedents explain his scholarly traits, his courtly bearing and his genius for leadership.

He was a skillful etcher and engraver and knew how to "make money"—in the literal sense. He had executive ability and planned his criminal forays like a general plotting a military campaign or a Wall Street banker directing a market coup.

In later years, Anderson was overshadowed by the more spectacular exploits of his pupil, Gerald Chapman, but those who knew insisted "Dutch" was the real brains of the gang.

It was a versatile group he gathered about him. Each was a specialist in some line of law-breaking. The mob would pull a bank job, then confuse the police by switching to forgery or wholesale passing of bogus money, with perhaps a holdup sandwiched in.

About Anderson's Dr. Jekyll–Mr. Hyde personality hangs many a tale. One had to do with his discovery in Spain that on one feast day of the year and only one, in a remote monastery ancient vestments, richly encrusted with jewels, were brought out for public display.

"Dutch" hatched a bold plan to raid the monastery on the feast day and steal the treasure. He gathered his mob in Paris a fortnight before the appointed day and then left for Rome, saying he would return in time for the Spanish monastery raid.

His mission in Rome was a bizarre one. He had picked up in Chicago an old volume of Latin which he translated. It contained a reference to an older, rarer book which Anderson longed to translate. He found that volume extant only in the library of the Vatican.

In Rome, he talked his way into the Vatican library and plunged into his translating.

The feast day came, the jeweled vestments were put on display, the people marveled at their richness and at night they were all put back into the monastery vaults.

In the meantime, the American mobsters waited impatiently for the leader who did not come. "Dutch" Anderson had become so engrossed in his Latin translation that he forgot all about the jewels, the plot to steal them and his waiting followers.

Chapman made a few "vacation" visits to Rochester with Anderson and Lawyer Baker's office was their rendezvous. Although they were unlike in many ways, the two criminals both went in for good literature. Anderson admired the works of Conrad and Oscar Wilde among the moderns. He could recite "The Ballad of Reading Gaol" by heart. Chapman fancied the verse of Amy Lowell.

Anderson tried to avoid gunplay and violence. The smoothly executed plan without the use of either was his objective. Chapman, the debonair French-Irishman, always carried a shooting iron and was at heart a killer.

Woman played little part in "Dutch's" life. But when "Chappy" came to town, he drove a flashy open car and he generally had a woman with him, seldom the same one twice. Everything about Gerald Chapman was showy. Anderson was the acme of good taste. He would fondle a rare book as a virtuoso would handle a fine old violin.

During their Rochester visits, the pair would down prohibition era firewater by the tumblerful. Anderson could handle his liquor well. "Chappy" would get noisy.

The pair liked to call themselves "Robin Hoods" who stole from the rich and gave to the poor. That was fantasy, although both were generous and some needy Rochesterians were recipients of their largess.

Anderson was the stronger, more intriguing figure of the two. Not that he was any paragon. He was a wicked man who did much evil in this world. It seems a pity he did not devote his talents to lawful pursuits and his artistic gifts to creative purposes. He might have attained a high place in the society he wasted his life fighting.

But he chose his own path. And in the end the highborn Ivan Dahl von Teller, the Heidelberg graduate who spoke four languages, died in a small-town alley in the foggy Michigan night—shot down like a hunted dog.

Chapter 20

"Pottsville" on the Genesee

Remember the "Mr. Tutt" stories by the late Arthur Train?

Their hero was a lanky old lawyer, a composite Uncle Sam and Abe Lincoln who wore Congress shoes and a stove pipe hat, who championed the underdog in court and confounded his rivals by citing some obscure point of law.

Many of the Tutt stories were placed in an upstate county seat village, full of quaint characters, called Pottsville. Train painted a word picture of the "smutty little wooden railroad station, the memorial library of funeral granite, the horse trough in the middle of Main Street, the beautiful old court house" in "The Hermit of Turkey Hollow" and other stories.

Did you know that Geneseo, home of the Wadsworths and the Genesee Valley Fox Hunt, is the prototype of the provincial Pottsville of the Mr. Tutt stories?

Through many of the pages strides the burly, homespun figure of Sheriff Moses Higgins, whose enforcement is diluted with a strong mixture of the milk of human kindness.

That sheriff was lifted from real life in the Genesee Valley. Author Train modeled his fictional character after George H. Root, onetime Livingston County sheriff and Avon businessman.

How this all came about goes back to the Fall of 1914 and one of the most famous court trials in Livingston County annals.

Train told much of the story in his book, "My Day in Court," a record of his own unusual career. For he was not only a writer of wide renown but also a lawyer, who in his younger days established a name as a skillful investigator and prosecutor.

In 1913 he was named a special prosecutor on the staff of Charles S. Whitman, then district attorney of New York County and soon to become governor.

Train's first important assignment was the prosecution of Henry Siegel, New York merchant-banker, charged with grand larceny after the collapse of his manifold enterprises, including private banks in New York and Boston and stores in New York, Chicago and other cities.

A Lilliputian figure, a little over five feet in height and weighing 115 pounds, Siegel was a German Jew who came to America at the age of 15 and fought his way up from a $3-a-week errand boy to the seats of the financial mighty. With his partner, Henry Vogel, he controlled at one time a dozen separate but affiliated enterprises. Depositors in his banks were principally Jewish sweatshop workers and his own not overpaid employes.

For years the Siegel businesses had actually been insolvent but had been kept alive by clever doctoring of the books and other devices to cover up the transfer of large sums from the banks to the stores. The inevitable crash came in 1913 and the little man found himself fighting for his freedom, virtually alone. His partner had died.

Siegel had retained as counsel one of the titans of the New York bar, John B. Stanchfield, onetime Democratic candidate for governor. A native of Elmira, in his youth he had been a star baseball player known throughout Western New York.

Knowing that feeling was running high in New York City, especially on the East Side where so many of Siegel's depositors lived, Stanchfield moved for a change of venue to his home county of Chemung. Whitman, aware of Stanchfield's popularity in the Elmira region, opposed such a move, just as his rival had foreseen. So the defense lawyer suggested Livingston County. Whitman agreed and the trial was set for Geneseo in early November of 1914. Livingston County had been Stanchfield's objective all the time.

In New York Train immediately began careful preparations for the trial. For months he had a firm of Scottish accountants, three legal assistants and a staff of detectives digging into every detail of Siegel's transactions.

One Summer day in 1914, a slight built, keen-eyed man dropped off a train at Geneseo's "smutty little railroad station." Arthur Train had come to the Genesee Valley to "spy out the ground," as he put it.

Here the sheriff enters the picture. Train immediately

struck up a friendship with broad-shouldered, sandy-haired, genial George Root. Train's book refers to him as "my firm friend, the sheriff, who later figures repeatedly in my stories."

The prosecutor knew that the right kind of a jury was vital to the success of his case. A special panel of 100 had been drawn for possible service in the Siegel trial. So, accompanied by the sheriff, who knew everybody from Fowlerville to East Avon by his first name, Train toured Livingston County from corner to corner, getting acquainted with every talesman. Thus he was able to compile a card index of the prejudices and beliefs of every potential Siegel juror.

As the day for opening of the trial neared, excitement mounted in the county seat. Huge moving vans, laden with records seized in Siegel's offices, rolled up to the handsome old court house. Reporters, some of them the stars of the New York press, flocked into town. Hordes of depositors, city-bred people with accents strange to the bucolic Valley, arrived and at once split into wrangling groups.

Train, in a letter to me in 1943, recalled "the fights between the depositor committees, often winding up with duckings in the horse trough." That circular concrete watering trough, with its fountain and bear statue, the gift to the village of one of the Wadsworths and an object of local pride, seems to have been imprinted on the author's memory. For in his Pottsville stories, the "horse trough" often bobs up.

When the trial opened on Nov. 9, the village's few

176

hotels were crammed to the eaves. Rooms in private homes were at a premium. There was a sound of revelry by night. Train's book tells how "the brilliantly lighted offices in the court house rattled to the sound of the ivories," testifying to the presence of the Fourth Estate. The late Dallas Newton, Geneseo and Rochester attorney who was associated with the defense counsel, recalled that the visiting scribes and lawyers "learned something about the Valley brand of poker."

The case of The People vs Henry Siegel opened before a packed court room. The hunting squires of the Valley and their ladies were there, along with the yeomanry.

The scene was surcharged with drama. There was the diminutive defendant whose feet barely touched the floor as he sat up front, a forlorn figure. There was Lawyer Stanchfield in cutaway, well creased trousers, a carnation in his buttonhole and exuding an air of big city prosperity.

Train wrote that despite Stanchfield's upstate origin and youthful baseball exploits, "there was little about him in 1914 to appeal to a country jury. He looked like a metropolitan bridegroom."

He added that when "Siegel was brought to the bar for trial before 12 straw-chewing rustics from Geneseo, Livonia, Mount Morris, Nunda, Groveland, West Sparta and Conesus, I wore my oldest clothes."

Train exaggerated the rural makeup of the jury. There were, it is true, ten farmers in the box but there also were a sophisticated horseman from Avon who had a business in

Rochester and a well-to-do Dansville nurseryman who was no "straw-chewing rustic."

And Dallas Newton, describing Train's personal appearance, spoke of him as "rather dapper." Even in his "oldest clothes," the prosecutor could not disguise his New York brand.

The case was a complicated one, involving a maze of financial statistics. Stanchfield's technique was to confuse the jury in this labyrinth of figures.

Train sought to put the case into terms the dullest farmer could understand. In his opening address he compared Siegel's trickery to the deceit practiced by a man who sells a horse through a false statement. For dollars he substituted bushels of wheat or tons of hay. He talked in terms the ruralite could grasp.

Former employes of Siegel testified, some with obvious reluctance, of the devious methods of the tiny defendant whose face grew longer as the trial progressed. Stanchfield soon saw he was fighting a losing battle. Toward the end, the defense virtually ceased to contest the facts and concentrated on an attack on the law. It closed its case abruptly after calling 10 character witnesses to the stand.

One reporter described Train's summation as "a most dramatic presentation."

"Had Siegel been a man," thundered the prosecutor, turning to the defendant, "he would have gone into bankruptcy long ago. But instead, with his dirty enterprises in mind, he allowed the middle class people, as Mr. Stanchfield has called them, to put money in the bank that he might flood it into his stores. Within eight days, there wasn't a penny of a shop girl too insignificant to be placed in his hands."

At 7:30 on the night of Nov. 22, Supreme Court Justice William W. Clark gave the case to the jury, declaring that he held serious doubts as to the validity of the grand larceny charge and virtually directing a verdict of guilty to a lesser count.

Everyone expected an early verdict. But as the hours passed and no word came from the jury room, the judge directed the sheriff to inquire if there was likelihood of an agreement. The sheriff returned with the laconic report that "the jury has not yet reached a verdict." Justice Clark set 11:30 as a deadline by which the jury must either reach a verdict or be locked up for the night.

What followed is told by Train in "My Day in Court" and "The Hermit of Turkey Hollow."

He recalled that the sheriff came to him and said: "Follow me." They made their way to the rear of the court house and up a flight of back stairs to what was apparently an attic directly over the jury room.

Let Train go on with the story:

"The attic was dusty, hot and full of cobwebs. Below all was silence, penetrated by an occasional hiss and punctuated now and then by a curse. What had occurred? Was there in fact a deadlock? After what seemed an incredible period of time, a chair scraped and a voice was heard:

" 'What time is it now, Bill?'

"There was a momentary hiatus during which a watch

179

evidently was consulted and then the foreman made reply: 'Eleven twenty.'

"Again the cloak of silence descended until I was startled by the voice of the foreman evidently just beneath.

" 'Wal, boys,' he sighed in a voice of relief, 'I reckon we kin claim another day's pay. After all three dollars is real money—wuth gettin! . . .'"

Train and the sheriff hastened to the court room in time to hear the jury foreman report a verdict of misdemeanor in that Siegel "obtained credit on false financial statements."

The little man was sentenced to serve 10 months in the Monroe County Penitentiary. The sentence was suspended for two months to give him a chance to make restitution to his creditors.

When he was unable to raise the money in the allotted time, the former millionaire became a resident of Rochester for eight months and ten days—in the old red brick penitentiary on South Avenue which was built in the pre-Civil War reign of Franklin Pierce.

After Siegel, a widower, had served his time, he married the woman who had been in charge of the telegraph office at Geneseo and who, Train said, "was the only person who had shown him any kindness during his miserable experience."

Siegel died within a few years, a heartbroken man who still believed that if the depositors had let him alone for a little while, he could have started all over again and paid them back.

Here is what Author Train wrote about Geneseo in "My Day in Court":

"The Geneseo (sic) Valley is, as is apt to be the case in localities where the population is stable, adheres to the land, marries within sight of its own chimneys, full of odd and picturesque characters.

"Here I encountered aristocratic neer-do-wells, tramps, gypsies, hermits, cranky old bachelors, misers, crooked politicians and all the usual prototypes of a New England village.

"Indeed the town of Geneseo itself, with its ramshackly buildings dating from the Civil War period and earlier, with its circular horse trough and 'deepo' became the prototype of Pottsville, the scene of many of my Mr. Tutt stories. When the time came, I merely transplanted it to the Mohawk Valley."

Local pride may impel some residents of the "Northern Bluegrass" to quarrel with Arthur Train's picture of their historic shire town.

They may find a crumb of comfort in these words from a letter the author wrote me in an almost illegible scrawl:

"As to Geneseo, it is Pottsville only in size and New England flavor."

Arthur Train is dead but his Mr. Tutt stories will never die.

And the "horse trough" still stands proudly in the center of Geneseo.

181

Chapter 21

Hermit's Gold

The Hermit of Hermitage couldn't take it with him. When James Lewis Blodget perished in the flaming ruins of his lonely home, he had to leave behind his hoard of gold pieces, his farms, his mortgages and the other worldly accumulations that had made him the richest man in Wyoming County.

He left another sort of legacy—a wealth of stories and legends about his fantastic way of life which has made him part of the folklore of Western New York. No countryside knew a more eccentric or paradoxical character.

James Blodget was reputedly a millionaire. Certainly his fortune ran into six figures.

Yet he lived as simply as a lone prospector in Death Valley. He cooked his own meals, made his own woolen shirts, washed his clothes and his dishes in the stream that purred by his kitchen door. He dressed like a penniless farm hand, in patched overalls, soiled denim jumper, broad-brimmed felt hat and, rain or shine, rubber boots.

He was a banker and handled large sums of money. He

7. John L. Sullivan Who Trained at Belfast

8. Leonard and Clara Jerome, Churchill's Grandparents

owned many farms, held mortgages on many others, besides possessing real estate in Rochester and Buffalo.

He was of pioneer stock. His father, Lewis Blodget, settled in Hermitage, south of Warsaw, in 1812. Besides possessing the acquisitive instinct, the senior Blodget, through marriage to Betsy Cravath, daughter of an early settler, inherited saw and grist mills, a tannery and several farms.

So the boy who was born in Hermitage in 1822 had unusual advantages for the times. A strapping six footer of 25, he entered Yale College and graduated in three years. He was awarded the wooden spoon emblematic of the highest scholastic standing in his class. He excelled in mathematics and engineering and for a year after his graduation taught math at Yale.

Then, after a visit to Washington, he returned to his native village to help his father in his many enterprises. Hermitage then was a self-sustaining trading center, not the somnolent, off-the-beaten path hamlet it is today.

James fell in love with a neighbor's daughter, a village belle. They became engaged and on a hill above the town slowly rose the mansion he was building for his affianced. The new house had been enclosed and painters had begun to streak its sides with white when one twilight Blodget's fiancee and a girl friend climbed the hill to look over the place.

They little knew that Blodget was in the building, also on a tour of inspection. He started to greet them when he overheard from his sweetheart's lips words that warped his whole future. As the story goes, he heard the girl say to her companion:

"I'll make his money fly after I marry him."

Blodget confronted his fiancee and ended their troth then and there. The next morning he discharged every workman on the job. He never entered the house again. Kegs of nails, boxes of glass, window frames stayed there, untouched. Until it fell into ruins, the unfinished house remained just as it had been the night of James Blodget's disillusionment.

All the rest of his life, he could see the abandoned, uncompleted house on the hill, the symbol of his blasted dreams. The girl of the story went West and married.

Blodget seemed to draw within himself and devoted his tremendous energy to making money. Despite his cultural background, the wealthiest taxpayer in the Town of Wethersfield hated the thought of paying school taxes and complained that "other people produce the children and I have to pay for their education."

Because he chose to visit his farms on foot, often striding crosslots through woods and swamps, wading streams, he resented having to pay for the upkeep of highways "other people used." He "worked out" his road tax rather than pay cash. He performed the hardest manual labor, chopped and hauled his own wood, shingled his buildings, dug ditches, mended his fences.

After the death of his father, he lived with his mother in an old yellow house with its living rooms built over tannery vats.

Four times robbers were lured to Hermitage by tales of Blodget's ill-guarded treasure and his solitary habits. Once they fled, empty handed. Twice bandits beat him when he was an old man.

Early one morning in 1875, while his mother was still living, three men broke into the house. They bound and gagged Blodget in his bed. One stood guard over him while another held a gun at the head of the aged mother and a third rifled the old wooden safe of between $12,000 and $20,000.

After the bandits left, Blodget managed to free himself and spread the alarm. Villagers followed the tracks of a buggy to a wood where the getaway vehicle had been abandoned. After more than a year, a man with a $500 bill in his possession was arrested, admitted he was one of the trio in the Blodget crime. He was convicted and served 12 years in prison. His confederates never were caught.

Blodget soon bought a huge "burglar-proof" safe with thick doors, a steel vault and a time lock which he installed in a two-story frame building. Residents began to leave their savings with him and he became a banker. His integrity was never questioned and his accounts were meticulously kept.

One night in 1899, villagers saw a light in the Blodget bank and discovered two men working on the safe. The banker was awakened and, armed with a club, led his fellow townsmen into his office. The yeggs fled out the rear door but not before the 77-year-old Blodget had clipped one of them with his bludgeon. He refused to pursue the pair beyond the bridge in the village. His safe and its contents were intact.

On July 4, 1904, three bandits invaded Blodget's bedroom, beat him and escaped with his watch and $20 in cash. They looked in vain for the gold he was thought to have secreted in the house.

On Nov. 4, 1904, Hermitage was awakened by a mighty explosion. Three yeggs, probably city professionals, had blown the Blodget bank safe wide open and, cowing aroused villagers with their revolvers, escaped with their loot, the amount of which Blodget would not reveal. It was believed to total $22,000. Before cracking the safe, the gang had visited Blodget's home and clubbed the 82-year-old banker into insensibility. Thereafter Blodget did most of his business by drafts on New York banks.

It was Blodget money that gave birth to Kenmore, thriving Buffalo suburb. An ambitious Hermitage youth went into the real estate business in Buffalo and got the idea of developing Kenmore, in the 1880s nothing but barren flat land. He came home, got his father interested in his idea and together they went to Blodget, seeking a large loan. The banker agreed to put up the money but insisted on the young promoter's father giving security on the loan. In the end Blodget got his money back, with interest, and lived to see Kenmore grow into a little city.

The banker was something of a showman. He delighted in amazing rural folk by working out involved mathematical problems in white chalk on the floor of his office.

He spent $500 for the latest works on electricity, which

joined the other scientific volumes, the biographies and the classics which filled his shelves. Reading was his only recreation. An agnostic who knew his Paine and Ingersoll, he could hold his own in any theological argument with the village dominies. No preacher called on him more than once.

Blodget was abstemious in all his habits. None of his money went for grog or tobacco. He was never profane. It was said his old mother had to smoke her clay pipe surreptitiously for fear of his displeasure.

For funerals or state occasions he would trim his scraggly beard and doff his worn work clothes for his one good suit, which was of the best material. Thus groomed, his tall powerful figure and erect bearing gave him a rather distinguished appearance. He would put on his good suit sometimes when he made business trips to Buffalo or Rochester. More often he'd go just the way he was, in his work clothes.

On one such visit to Rochester, according to a story which probably is apocryphal, Blodget entered a smart store and began nosing around. A clerk, thinking his visitor a bum, asked him to leave. Whereupon James L. Blodget said with quiet dignity:

"Young man, I happen to own this property."

He would overpay workmen in sudden spells of generosity. But if a solicitor for some cause approached him, he would receive a brusque refusal.

If a farmer gave Blodget a lift, the banker sometimes would pay for food for man and beast at the next hotel. He might even hand over a dollar. In a few days, he might be asking that same man for an interest payment and if the amount happened to be $23.01, the money lender would never throw off the extra penny.

Once a man came to the Blodget bank, saying with assurance: "I have been on that farm 20 years now and have never made a payment on it. By the law of squatter sovereignty the place is now mine." Blodget went to his safe, rummaged through his papers and came back with one, saying: "It recites here that the first year you were on that farm, I had you draw me a load of wood. I put that down as a payment. The 20 years are not up yet and I guess you had better move."

Seldom did Blodget foreclose. He would visit a farmer whose mortgage was about to expire, timing his appearance with the noon meal. In the hospitable tradition of the countryside, the visitor would be asked to break bread with the family. Then the banker would record the payment of 50 cents on the debt and keep the mortgage alive.

When the Buffalo, Rochester & Pittsburgh Railway, now part of the B. & O. system was built, the first surveys ran through Hermitage. Blodget did not want a railroad in his village, fearing it would bring tramps to rob him. So he used his influence to swing the tracks from Warsaw to Bliss via Hardy's instead of Hermitage. Some of his neighbors never quite forgave him for depriving their village of a place on the railroad.

A classic Blodget yarn is about the wheelbarrow ride he gave Will Strickland. The banker overheard Will say on a street corner: "I'd give a dollar to be in Wethersfield Springs now." The banker said: "I'll take you there for half that amount, cash in advance."

Will handed over the half dollar. Blodget went to his barn and returned with a wheelbarrow of heroic size, in keeping with his great physical strength. Strickland got aboard. An accomplished harmonica player, he chanced to have his mouth organ in his pocket.

So as the Croesus of Wyoming County bent to the handles of the barrow, Will struck up a merry tune and the fantastic three-mile jaunt began—to musical accompaniment. The passenger reported later that Blodget set the barrow only once and then to take off his coat. It was a steaming hot day. At Wethersfield Springs, the rich man wheeled smartly up to the porch of the hotel and told his fare: "You're here. Get off."

On the night of Dec. 6, 1905, Blodget stopped in a village store for a chat before going to his lonely home. Sometimes he was garrulous. Again he would work with other men for hours without uttering a word.

Just after midnight a villager saw the Blodget house wrapped in flames. He spread the alarm but the crowd that gathered could do nothing. The place was a raging furnace.

The next morning, while the ruins were still smoking, men began a hunt for the banker's body. One searcher picked up a $20 gold piece. It was literally "hot money." The search for the remains of James Blodget was halted as men burned their hands, scooping up coins.

Then Dr. George Blackmer of Silver Springs, Blodget's

189

nephew, arrived on the scene. In tones of authority, he reminded the money hunters they were taking property that did not belong to them and ordered them to return what they had found. Shamefacedly, they emptied their pockets into a water pail until it held more than a peck of coins. The hunt for the hermit's body was resumed. It was found, charred beyond recognition, in a corner of the cellar.

There was some talk of foul play but an investigation indicated that the fire had started from an overheated stove or a defective chimney.

The Blodget fortune eventually passed to a niece. The strange, lonely man who had piled it up was laid to rest in the village burying ground. But still the stories persist of the Yale graduate who patched his own overalls.

Chapter 22

Lost in a Salt Mine

"Have they got Floyd Collins out of that cave yet?"

Remember those February days of 1925 when that question was on every lip as the nation watched the epic struggle for the life of an obscure youth, trapped in the narrow passageway of a Kentucky sand cave, with a seven-ton boulder pinning his foot?

Remember how after 17 tension-packed days, the body of Floyd Collins was left in its tomb?

That story became a virtual American saga. Songs and poems have been written about it—but not lately.

Western New York has its own strange story of a youth being imprisoned in the depths of the earth. It was not a national sensation. It inspired no songs or poetry. In fact curiously little was written about it.

Yet for many August days in 1916, people up Retsof way were asking this one question.

"Have they found Benny Seduskie in that mine yet?"

Over the hills 30 miles southwest of Rochester is one of the largest rock salt mines in the world, that of the International Salt Co. at a place called Retsof, the name of a onetime mine owner spelled backward. There for more than 80 years men have been blasting the salt out of the bed of a prehistoric lake.

There 1,000 feet down and under three villages, Restof, Greigsville and Wadsworth, is a veritable city of white walled catacombs, of pillared chambers through which twist miles of "streets" and narrow gauge tracks. Once mules which never saw the light of day hauled the salt cars down the tracks. For many years electric locomotives have done the job.

For 12 days and 12 nights, 21-year-old Benny Seduskie was lost in that labyrinth. He had wandered without food or water, in the dank blackness, some of the time crawling on his hands and knees, hoping to find the path to freedom—after nine tortured days he sank to the ground, waiting rescue or the end of time for him.

Benny was a big, blond Russian who had drifted in, from nobody knew where, to work in the Retsof mine less than a year earlier. He had no kin in the mining village—actually none in America—and no intimates. He was working as a helper on a drilling machine that fateful Saturday night of August 12, 1916.

The night shift's work was done and Benny was making his way to the foot of the shaft, for some reason behind the other workers. The carbide lamp on his cap went out. In a few minutes the power was switched off and the mine was plunged into darkness. That meant the other men had reached the top of the shaft in the elevator. No one had missed the lagging Benny.

He had no matches. He thought he could find his way to the shaft. When he was nearly there, he made a wrong turn. He veered to the right, following railway tracks until he came to a locomotive. He sat there a while, trying to get his bearings. Then he continued his mistaken course eastward until he was in an abandoned part of the mine.

Benny had a package of tobacco in his pocket and he rationed it, a few grains at a time, sucking in the moisture until it was gone. Then he became wild with thirst. In the distance he could hear the rat-a-tat-tat of the drills, the boom of the blasting and the drone of the locomotives. Desperately he tried to direct his faltering steps toward the sounds. But he could not find the right road.

For nine days he wandered, sometimes in circles, in ever mounting agony, physical and mental. He took some blasting wire from his pocket and tied it about his waist, tightening it as the hunger pains increased.

He lost all track of time. Day and night were the same in his dungeon. At first he had shouted for help but soon gave that up, to conserve his strength. He slept when overcome by exhaustion.

When he became too weak to stand, he crawled. Those pitiful feet and hand prints were found later. When Benny finally sank to the mine floor, he was only 60 feet from the main gangway, the pathway to freedom.

The hunt began two days after he was lost in the mine and failed to show up at his boarding place. At first the

Livingston County sheriff and his men searched nearby woods and a reservoir.

Then, when no one could be found who had seen Benny since the night of August 12 and no workman remembered his coming out of the mine, searching parties went underground. The hunters split into parties of three or four men and each group fanned out in different directions. Tension grew in the countryside as the days went by and the search went on and still no trace of the big Russian.

Fred S. Mosele, in charge of electrical work in the mine, had a sudden hunch that Benny had strayed off into the abandoned part of the mine. He, Deputy Sheriff William Mann and Constable William Simpson poked around on the east side for an hour and one half and were about to call it quits when Mosele heard a faint sound, a sort of hollow moan.

A moment later all three men heard the moan. They dashed in the direction whence it came. Mosele was the first to see Seduskie. The miner, thin as a skeleton and black as a newly polished stove, was struggling to rise. He was too weak to stand and was carried to the main shaft. The elevator he had missed 12 days earlier took him up from his dank prison into the fresh air.

Twilight was dappling the rolling hills of the Genesee Valley that August 25 of 1916 when Benny Seduskie was rescued. He weighed only 90 pounds when he was taken out of his "tomb." When he went into the mine August 12 he had weighed nearly 180 pounds. The first thing the Russian asked for was a cigaret.

Benny was put under a physician's care and laid on a cot in the company's offices. The doctor said "No visitors," as word of the rescue spread throughout the countryside.

He was to be given a teaspoonful of whiskey and a teaspoonful of milk every half hour during the night. Toward dawn, after the doctor had left and the two men on guard were dozing, Benny managed to get up and drink his fill of ice water from a pan. He was made of tough fiber, that Russian, for he seemed to suffer no ill effects. The next day he was brought to a Rochester hospital. He was released in a few weeks, fully recovered—at least physically.

When Benny returned to the Retsof area—but never to the salt mine—he had served in the Army in World War I. The draft had caught him but, so far as known, he had no harrowing battle experience.

But people, who had known him before his entombment in the catacombs, noticed a great change in the big youth who had been good natured and quiet. The new Benny was quarrelsome, erratic and given to drinking sprees.

Those who knew of his ordeal in the mine understood.

Old clippings from Valley newspapers record that on the night of August 16, 1923, just seven years after he had been wandering, lost in the salt mine, Benjamin Seduskie, then residing in Nunda, rode, in a truck which he had commandeered at gunpoint, to the Retsof home of Douglas Johns for whom he had worked.

Benny started an argument with Johns about money.

195

Clarence Mitchell, 24, a boarder in the Johns home, heard the loud voices and tried the role of peacemaker. Benny shot him to death.

In the archives of the stately old Court House at Geneseo, it is recorded that:

"On November 19, 1923, Benjamin Seduskie was indicted for murder in the first degree. He was arraigned and pleaded not guilty. Thereafter, on November 21, 1923, he pleaded guilty to murder in the second degree and was sentenced to Auburn State Prison for not less than 20 years nor more than life."

So the doors of a surface prison clanged shut behind Benny Seduskie, who once had been imprisoned for 12 days in the depths of the earth.

Chapter 23

The Linden Murders

This is a murder mystery tale from real life. The characters are not rich, famous or glamorous. They are plain country folk. The setting is not a baronial castle or an exotic isle. It is a hamlet in Genesee County named Linden, off the beaten path and unknown even to most regional residents until the spotlight swung on it in the early 1920s.

Twice within 18 months a maniacal killer struck in this settlement of less than 100 people and four persons, all middle-aged and none with a known enemy, were slain, brutally and without reasonable motive.

The Linden murders must go down as the most baffling in modern Western New York crime annals, particularly because investigators were generally agreed that the slayer was a resident of the community, although they never could break any suspect down.

First, we must go back to late October of 1922, the time of harvest, when the orchards were red with ripened fruit along the road from Bethany to Linden, villages whose names betray their New England origin.

On that road, one and one half miles from Linden, Frances Leora Kimball, 72-year-old spinster, lived in an old fashioned frame house where her parents had lived and died. It was a snug little farm of 60 acres where Miss Kimball lived with her bachelor brother, Willie.

On Monday, Oct. 22, 1922 at 10 A.M., Willie left for his work in a fruit warehouse. There he spent the night as was his custom in the busy harvest season.

Franc Kimball was a raw-boned, hard working woman. Her tongue may have been a bit sharp at times but she minded her own business, had a limited circle of friends and lived at peace in the family homestead. She was a woman of fixed routine. Promptly at 6 each evening she milked her cow.

Mid-afternoon of Oct. 23, a farmer neighbor noticed that the Kimball cow had not been milked. Seeing no signs of life about the place, he became alarmed and called the state police. The gray riders found the front door locked. They battered it down.

Accompanied by neighbors, they began to search the house. In the cellar a farmer saw a foot protruding from under a potato bin.

The body of Frances Kimball had been jammed under a shelf and partly covered with an old door. Her head had been battered. The weapon was a stone found nearby.

There were few signs of a struggle. Her clothing was little disarranged. A fruit jar had been tipped over a shelf. A pan of eggs, which she had evidently just gathered before she was struck down, was found nearby—with a few blood spots on them. There were bloodstains also on a piece of lumber. The house had not been ransacked. There was no indication of robbery. And there were no clues to the killer.

The police theorized that the slayer entered through an outside cellar hatchway, first knocked Miss Kimball unconscious with his fist, then finished her off with the rock. Then the killer bolted the door between the cellar and the first floor, walked out the front door, locking it and either taking the key with him or tossing it away. It never was found.

The intruder did a strange and seemingly needless thing. He cut a telephone wire, just outside the cellar window, apparently with a jack knife. A few weeks before, there had been an attempt to burglarize the Linden store and a wire had been cut there in the same fashion.

The victim's brother, Willie, proved to the investigators' complete satisfaction that he had spent the night in the warehouse. He was stunned by the tragedy.

A motorist came forward with a story of seeing an elderly but burly and roughly clad stranger walking near the Kimball home on the afternoon before the body was found. The man had been slashing at the grass along the road as he stalked along.

The manhunters rounded up all the tramps, migrants and hermits they could find in Western New York. Scores were brought in and questioned. It was all to no avail.

Franc Kimball went to her grave with her slayer still at large. Excitement ran high in a countryside unused to acts of violence. Who would murder a defenseless old farm woman for no apparent reason?

The troopers and Genesee County sheriff deputies doggedly followed every lead. At the end of a month they had to give up.

But there had been a witness to the crime. When neighbor women came to the Kimball home after the discovery of the tragedy, Mugs, the spinster's pet cat, meowed in piteous fashion and hid under a sofa. If only Mugs could talk!

It was March, that madcap month that badgers and taunts York Staters just before the coming of the Spring. Nearly 18 months had gone by since the Kimball murder. The country folk were just beginning to breathe easier and the excited buzzing of little groups had almost died away in little Linden.

Then the killer struck again. The date was March 11, 1924.

At 6 o'clock each evening, 50-year-old Mabel Howard Morse, who kept the village store while her husband, George, a traveling man, was on the road, went down the street a few doors to a neighbor's home for milk.

That neighbor was Thomas Whaley. He was 55, a section hand on the Erie Railroad, a stone's throw from his home, where he lived with his wife, aged 55. The Whaleys were quiet, hard-working, respectable people with no surplus of the world's goods.

When after an hour, Mrs. Morse failed to return to the store, three men, waiting there and knowing her routine, became worried. They went to the Whaley house and found all the doors locked. One of them raised a kitchen window. From it emerged a wisp of smoke.

The men broke down a rear door. In a first floor bedroom they found three bodies piled in what had been intended for a funeral pyre. An oil-soaked rug had been thrown over them, oil had been dashed on the carpets and on the bed but only a smoldering fire had resulted.

The Whaleys had been shot to death and Mrs. Morse killed with a pick-axe handle. There were blood stains on the kitchen floor, two bullet marks in the kitchen woodwork, three 32-caliber revolver shells on the floor but no sign of a gun.

An overturned chair and a pitcher of milk on the kitchen table, set for the evening meal, indicated that the Whaleys had been killed in the kitchen and then dragged into the bedroom.

The key of the front door was missing and the rear door was bolted. The Whaleys had no telephone wire to cut. The hand of the Kimball slayer was written all over this triple murder.

As the crime was reconstructed, it was deduced that the slayer entered the Whaley home through an outside cellar hatchway, shot Mrs. Whaley first. Her husband, doing his chores in the barn, heard the shot, picked up the pick-axe handle and came charging in.

Tom Whaley was not lacking in physical courage. It was deduced that the murderer fired one wild shot as Whaley circled the kitchen, another as he dodged into the pantry and then sent a bullet into the section hand's neck.

Then Mrs. Morse came in with her milk pail, saw the gory spectacle and was struck down with the pick handle. Was she an unintended victim or did the killer, knowing her routine, wait for her in the darkened home? At any rate, he at some time pulled down the shades, covered one window with a blanket and started the fire which he hoped would obscure his crime.

Next he bolted the outside cellar door, went upstairs, locked the back door of the house, went out the front door, locking it and taking the key with him. It was the Kimball murder mystery all over again, only this time there were three victims, instead of one.

Whaley's empty pocketbook and two empty purses belonging to his wife were found. Two watches were missing. The obvious motive was robbery. But the more experienced investigators did not believe the slayer would risk his life for such small booty. In the end the manhunters were almost unanimous in their belief that their quarry was a resident of the neighborhood, a cunning man with a twisted mind, probably with sadistic tendencies. None of the female victims had been molested sexually.

As in the Kimball case, there was a sweeping roundup of tramps and strays. One of them, a paroled convict, confessed the murder one day, repudiated it the next and was found to have been 25 miles away at the time of the murder. Eventually all those rounded up had to be released.

Reporters from Buffalo and Rochester newspapers flocked into little Linden. They made the county seat, Batavia, 14 miles from the murder scene, their headquarters and taxicab drivers never had it so good. Each reporter had his or her solution to the tragedy.

The late George S. Brooks, who later became a fiction writer for magazines and a script writer for Hollywood, in 1924 was a police reporter for the old *Rochester Herald*. George invented a "wild man" who lived in the woods. His stories made good reading but the cops could find no "wild man" in any woods near Linden.

The fear-stricken townspeople were questioned but none threw any light on the mystery. It was strange that in a hamlet, where everyone's movements are common property, no one had been seen entering the Whaley house. Stranger still was the fact that no one had heard the shots although the spot was by no means isolated.

The investigators and reporters came upon many things that were strange about Linden, which had overnight become an armed camp.

For the first time in their lives, residents bolted their doors. Rusty fire-arms were dragged out from attics and placed within easy reach. Clairvoyants were consulted. One woman fainted when a neighbor on a casual errand rapped at her door. There were rumblings in the hills that the white robed Knights of the Ku Klux Klan, then in their heyday in the area, would take a hand in the case. They didn't.

There was fear in every heart. Who knew when and where the murderer in their midst would strike again?

State Troopers, their gray uniforms spattered with mire, rode on horseback over the countryside. Cars of investigators became mired in the hub-deep mud of the roads. A veritable army of sensation hunters descended on the once tranquil hamlet.

After two months of wild rumors, hectic dashes hither and yon and questioning of scores, the manhunt came to a dead end.

Gradually peace returned to Linden.

But the maniac who slew four innocent persons is still at large. By now he may have joined his victims in the Great Beyond.

Chapter 24

The Last Sextuplet

So many things come in lots of six. For instance there's the handy "six pack" in the beverage department.

But seldom do babies come in lots of six. In fact it has happened but SIX times in recorded medical history.

A Dr. Hellin, who researched the statistics of multiple births, wrote that odds against quadruplets were 6 million to 1 and of quintuplets 500 million to 1. As to sextuplets, he gave no ratios but observed that "sextuplets represent the limit of human multiple births."

All of these statistics are leading up to the fact that America's last sextuplet lived for half a century in Wyoming County.

Her name was Mrs. Alincia Bushnell Parker and it was my privilege to chat with her in 1949 at Silver Lake, where she lived for 47 of her 88 years.

The next Spring she left her lakeshore cottage for a nursing home in the village of Wyoming. There she died in 1952.

Mrs. Parker showed me a jealously guarded document

dated "Chicago, Sept. 15, 1866" and signed by Dr. James Edwards, attending physician and Miss Pissila Bancroft, midwife and nurse. That paper, proving her claim to fame, read:

"This to certify that Mrs. Jennie A. Bushnell, wife of J. I. Bushnell, in the city of Chicago on the 8th day of September, 1866, gave birth to six living children, three girls and three boys."

The boys were named Alberto, Norberto and Loberto and the girls, Lucy, Alice and Alincia.

Loberto died in Chicago at the age of seven months and Lucy a month later. The four others lived on into the 20th Century. Norberto died in Buffalo in 1905: Alberto in Albion in 1940 and Alice Bushnell Hughes, wife of a minister, in Arizona in 1946.

Her death left stout-hearted Alincia, widow of Daniel Parker, the only sextuplet anywhere, so far as can be determined.

You remember the sensation the birth of the Dionne quintuplets in Canada created in 1934. Strange to say, the arrival of the Bushnell sextuplets received scant attention in 1866.

There was no radio to spread the astounding news. No newspaper syndicate rushed agents to Chicago to bid for exclusive story and picture rights. There was no silver screen on which the tiny figures could be seen by millions. No curious crowds traveled miles to the Bushnell home. Dr. Edwards, who delivered the six babies, got no publicity. You'll recall how Dr. Dafoe, the Canadian country physician, became a famous figure in the 1930s.

Alincia Parker did recall that when she was a young girl, she and her surviving brothers and sisters were offered a fancy price to appear in a circus and that her parents would have none of it, although her mother, a French-woman, had been an actress. Jennie Le Charlton married James Bushnell in Milwaukee.

He was a bookkeeper and when the children were young, the family came East from Chicago and he worked in Buffalo, Rochester, Lockport and Albion. In the two latter places he was employed by quarrying interests when that industry was at its peak along the Erie Canal.

Mrs. Parker told me some of her dimming memories of her girlhood in the Lockport area, of the great canal locks there and of a white horse she used to ride. In the early 1890s she married Daniel Parker and they went to live at Silver Lake, near the Methodist Assembly Grounds. It was a bustling place, a "little Chautauqua," in those days. The Parkers ran a little store and sold newspapers and other goods to the cottagers and hundreds of others who flocked to the pretty little lake in the green hills in the Sum-mertime.

After her husband's death, Mrs. Parker continued to live in a year-around cottage next door to the Silver Lake Post-office. For 35 years she walked every working day the four miles to and from her job in the Perry Knitting Mills. Some nights she would walk to Perry to see a movie and hike home after the show.

One night in 1947 when she was bound on foot to the movies in the village, she was run down by an automobile and seriously injured. She spent some time in a hospital and had to quit her job and her hikes.

But "Lincha," as her neighbors knew her, kept her own house and got to see the motion pictures occasionally, riding to Perry and back in friends' cars. The knitting mill management saw to it that she was supplied with free tickets to the shows.

"I guess show business is in my blood," she told me. "My mother was an actress, you know, and I've always liked all kinds of shows. If I could have had my way, I would have gone into the circus when in my childhood I had the chance."

We are getting ahead of our story. It was in 1930 that the white light of national publicity beat upon the widow of Silver Lake, although through the years some newspaper or magazine would dig up the story of the Bushnell sextuplets.

In 1930 the late Robert L. Ripley put Mrs. Parker in his "Believe It or Not" feature which appeared in newspapers from coast to coast. Not only that but he invited "Lincha" to visit New York, all expenses paid, as his guest.

Mrs. Parker's eyes shone as she told of those glorious ten days in the Big Town.

"Bob Ripley was so good to me. I rode both ways on the Pullman cars. I was on a nation-wide broadcast. I saw ten shows and went to six night clubs. I met Rudy Vallee,

Jackie Coogan, Beatrice Lillie, Bing Crosby and other famous folks. It was the greatest time of my whole life."

In 1934 out of the backwoods of Canada came the story of the birth of the five Dionne daughters and of the doctor who saved their lives. Again the old story of the Bushnell sextuplets was revived and Mrs. Parker basked in the reflected glory of the quintuplets.

"Some folks tried to cast doubt on our claim to being sextuplets," she said, her eyes misting a little. But she had her certificate and Ripley, who verified every one of his "Believe It or Nots," backed her up.

Dr. Dafoe became interested in the Western New York sextuplet and Mrs. Parker said he was arranging for her to visit the "quints" at the time of his death.

As long as she lived, the last of the sextuplets kept green her memories of her days of glory in New York when she met "the famous folks."

Chapter 25

"Yellowstone" Kelly

Luther Sage Kelly was the name given the boy who was born in the old town of Geneva on July 29, 1849.

But it was as "Yellowstone" Kelly, Indian fighter, Army scout, explorer and hunter, that he became a legendary figure whose adventures were portrayed on the silver screen and on television in recent years.

He was born in a house that stood at Pulteney Street and Elmwood Avenue, the present site of St. Stephen's Church.

His father, Luther Kelly, left his native New Hampshire to "go West," first to Chittenango, where he found his bride, Jeanette Sage, then pushed on to Geneva in 1822. He became a merchant and a one-time postmaster of the village.

The Kellys' sturdy, clear-eyed son attended Geneva's Union School and early in life displayed a fondness for the outdoors, roaming the hills and woods around Lake Seneca.

The boy wasn't much interested in books and not at all in the cultural tone the village had achieved after it became the site of a college and the home of many gentry.

The youth was only 16 when he enlisted in the Union Army, misrepresenting his real age because he wanted to have a part in the great war.

He served in Mississippi and in Dakota Territory in the waning months of the long conflict.

After the war, a detachment of his regiment was sent to Minnesota to put down an uprising of Indians who were raiding settlements.

By then the West was in his blood. He served as an Army scout under General Nelson A. Miles and fought warlike tribes led by such chiefs as Sitting Bull and Crazy Horse.

A superb horseman and a crack shot, his insignia was a bear's paw hung over his pony's saddle.

When he was not fighting Indians, he was exploring and hunting in the wildest parts of the West, alone on horseback. He became an authority on then uncharted regions such as the Yellowstone country, hence the nickname which forever after clung to him.

Kelly was in demand as a guide and a mapmaker. After peace was made with the Indians, the tribesmen were friendly to "Yellowstone." They trusted and respected him.

In 1878 he revisited the scenes of his boyhood. His family had left Geneva for Elmira. In the effete East, he was a conspicuous figure because of his fringed jacket and long hair.

His stay in the region of his nativity was brief. He found life in New York State dull and stifling and yearned for the open spaces of the West.

211

"Yellowstone" Kelly's life was crammed with adventurous action. He carried the mails across the wild Indian territory. He was a guide in a new frontier, Alaska, and as a captain of volunteers, served in the Philippine insurrection in the wake of the Spanish-American War.

Somewhere along the line he had written—or had someone write—his memoirs. The Geneva Historical Society has one of the rare copies of his autobiography.

He lived his last years as an orchardist in California, where he died in 1928 at the age of 79.

The old frontiersman was buried at Billings, Mont., in the Western country in which he had lived so long and so dangerously. The pinnacle on which his tombstone stands, enclosed by a fence and bearing a plaque, was renamed Kelly Mountain in honor of the famous native of Geneva, N.Y.